The Mind Al-Qur'an Builds

The Mind
Al-Qur'an
Builds

NEW EDITION

by
Syed Abdul Latif

Islamic Book Trust
Kuala Lumpur
2002

© Islamic Book Trust 2002
ISBN 983-9154-35-4

FIRST PUBLISHED 1952

THIS NEW EDITION 2002
Islamic Book Trust
607 Mutiara Majestic
Jalan Othman
46000 Petaling Jaya
Malaysia
Website: www.ibtbooks.com
Email: ibtkl@pd.jaring.my

REVISED AND EDITED BY
Mohamed El-Tahir El-Mesawi

COVER DESIGN BY
Bounce Graphics
bounce@tm.net.my

PRINTED BY
Academe Art & Printing Services
Kuala Lumpur

Contents

Preface		vii
1	The Qur'an in Medieval Bondage	1
2	The Moorings	10
3	The Equipment	27
4	The Will of God	42
5	*Al-'Amal al-Ṣāliḥ*	64
6	Life Hereafter	74
7	*Ummatun Waṣaṭ*	97
8	The Cultural Basis of Civilization	111
9	Prayers in Islam	123
Index		133

Preface

In the brief span of our own lifetime, we have experienced two world wars and are now as a matter of course looking forward to a third. It is true that those who came out victorious in the first, talked of ending all wars and created a machinery of peace, the League of Nations, and when that proved of no avail and they found themselves engaged in another war, a more serious affair than the first, and were triumphant again, they reverted to their talk of ending wars, and set up another machinery, the United Nations Organization, holding out the hope that things would improve and the world return to peace. That peace is still eluding us.

The achievements of science had shattered for us the old barriers of time and space and reduced this globe of ours into but a small house wherein even whispers could be heard from corner to corner. Never before was there so great an opportunity for mankind to come close together and demonstrate that they were all "Children of God" as Christ conceived, or one single family, the "Family of God"[1] as did the Prophet of Islam, "every man,

---

1 Editor's note: For a detailed discussion on the authenticity of this tradition and the different chains of its transmission, see Ismāʻīl bin Muḥammad al-ʻAjlūnī: *Kashf al-Khafāʼ wa Muzīl al-Albās*, Beirut: Dār Iḥyāʼ al-Turāth,

a brother unto every other".² And yet even this small house stands divided, a victim to two powerful conflicting forces, one represented by Soviet Russia, and the other by the USA, curiously both members of one and the same peace organization.

How long is this state of affairs to last? The conflict, it is stated, is one of ideologies. Is it so? Even like the American, the Soviet Bloc have their own vocabulary of peace, making its appeal to the same natural fear of war and wish for security. The Soviet rulers, even as those who hold the reins of Government on the other side, talk of people's democracy and profess to entertain a like distaste for imperialists and war-mongers. In either case, the professed objective is a higher standard of living for the common man. Given mutual good-will, it should not be impossible to reconcile two such ideologies as profess a common purpose. Indeed, if reconciliation on every detail is not possible, surely, the two systems can work side by side on the basis of tolerance and possible cooperation. And yet the organisation of the United Nations whose function it was to eliminate friction between its members and effect a rapprochement has so far made no visible move to bring about a reconciliation between the two. Under its very nose armaments are piling up every day in either camp. A 'cold war' is already on.

Frankly, this is no conflict in favour of the economic uplift

---

1351 H, *hadīth* no. 1220 (Vol. 1, p. 457).

2 *Sahīh al-Bukhārī*, Beirut: Dār al-Kutub al'Ilmiyyah, 1412/1992, 'Kitāb al-Mazālim', *hadīth* no. 2442 (vol. 2, part 3, p.137); *Sahīh Muslim*, ed. by Muhammad Fu'ād 'Abdul Bāqī, Beirut: Dār Ihyā' al-Turāth al-'Arabī, n.d., 'Kitāb al-Birr wa'l-Silah, *hadīth* no. 2580 (vol. 4, p.1996).

Preface

of the common man. In fact, there is no ideology involved here. At all events, the common man is not the centre of thought in either company. What is it all about then? I may not persuade myself to exclaim with the Duke of Albany in *King Lear*: "'Tis the times' plague, when mad men lead the blind". Still, my feeling is that the answer lies somewhere in the neighbourhood of that utterance. "The *Sālihīn* shall inherit the earth," (*Anbiyā'*, 21:105) says the Qu'ran, men who maintain poise in life and protect it from every form of exploitation. It is they who function as the 'Vicegerents of God' on earth and create and sustain therein the order that subsists in the Universe. Could it be that there is a dearth of this type in our midst? Could it be that the conflict is in truth a race between those who lead the blind?

The cult of nationalism is now stalking in the land with its emphasis on the interests of individual nations and its reluctance to spread that emphasis equably on the interests of mankind as whole. Interwoven with the texture of modern democracy, it has given a degraded aspect to the democratic principle of suffrage and thwarted the rise of *Sālihīn* to helm the affairs of every country, and in consequence prevented humanity from growing into the Prophet's vision of one world, of a fold "every member of which shall be a shepherd unto every other, and be accountable for the welfare of the fold". It is this shepherd mind that we need today to make a success of the UNO. Else, even this organization will go the way its forbears have gone, strutting for a while as but a clearing house of international espionage. The cause of unity and of civilization is crossed singly neither by capitalism nor by communism which is but a violent reaction to it, but by a hearty interaction of the two, both sustained and encouraged by the self-same spirit of nationalism.

The task of rooting out this evil or of humanizing it is a spiritual function; and it is for the religions of the world to show the way. Of late they have been relegated into the background, and in their place, the idol of secularism has been installed everywhere, as if secularism in any form can endure for long without some spiritual basis to it. That basis will have to be furnished by religion ultimately. Else, secularism divorced from spirituality will multiply the evils proceeding from nationalism and vitiate human life still further. A return to the unifying element in every religion is the only refuge for man today, and that is possible only when it is cleared of accretions. The unity of God stressed by religion, is according to the Qur'an, to express itself in the unity of man, or in a peaceful order of existence for man. That is its true role. It is for those who share this view to study and disclose the potentialities that lie latent in their several faiths to develop the shepherd mind the world needs, and create a band of *Ṣāliḥīn* in every part of the world who may conjointly endeavour to restore poise to human life and pave the way to one world.

Born to the faith of the Qur'an and grown in its atmosphere, it has been but natural for me, and easy to study the possibilities furnished by it to mould this shepherd mind for the world of today. Strictly speaking, my study is a study in introspection, a bringing to mind of the values of life which in the course of history have been very largely laid aside by my brethren in faith. The task has been undertaken in humility and in full consciousness of my limitations. In the pursuit of it, I confess, I have had to tread on delicate ground and try to negotiate with certain

Preface xi

deep-seated sentiments entertained by them. My only justification is my urge to lift, as far as I could, the veils that have been allowed to rest on the Qur'an, and to let it speak for itself unhindered any longer by its medieval associations. It is now for others better qualified but who are silent so far to take up this task, and correct and amplify and complete the picture which I have tried to delineate here of the mind which the Qur'an aims to mould for man.

In the preparation of the volume, I have received valuable help from two friends. One is an old colleague of mine on the staff of the Osmania University, Hyderabad, Allama Abdul Qadir Siddiqi, for long Head of the Faculty of Muslim Theology, a scholar for whose grasp of the Qur'anic knowledge I have always held a high regard. Representing as he does the old order of Muslim theologians, he, nevertheless, possesses the talent to enter into the minds of those who would like to make a fresh approach to the sources of theological knowledge. Consequently, I have received considerable encouragement from the sympathetic attitude which he has always displayed towards my lines of thought touching the leading issues of life raised by the Qur'an. The other friend to whom I am indebted is the present Curator of the Asafiyah State Library, Hyderabad, Dr Muhammad Rahatullah Khan, M.A. (Osmania), D. Phil (Leipzig). He may be accepted as a typical representative of the new order of Muslim scholars who are not quite in sympathy with our medieval heritage and are, at the same time, not well satisfied with the trends of modern civilization. The Doctor happens to be an old pupil of mine in the Department of English studies at the Osmania University, and has retained his old affection for his teacher. He has shown a deep insight into the difficulties of my undertaking and offered me every facility of reference and consultation in his library where most of my work was done. I feel happy to acknowledge that I have freely drawn upon his wide and varied knowledge of the Arabic literature which has been the main subject of his study.

Conscious as I am of my deep obligations to these two friends in the presentations of my thesis, it will be unfair on my part if I should let them share the responsibility that should attach to the expression of views such as have been advanced in this volume. For those views, I alone should be held responsible; for, indeed, they have grown with me and are today part of me.

In conclusion, I have to express my deep thanks to Dr Yusufuddin, Reader in 'Religion and Culture', Osmania University, for having added a carefully prepared index to the volume.

The regret is felt that, in the transliteration of Arabic terms and names, the diacritical type could not be used for lack of it at the moment.*

Syed Abdul Latif
Hyderabad, India
September 1952

---

* *Publisher's note: This edition uses the standard diacritical marks for Arabic pronunciation. Other changes include editor's notes on selected footnootes and references, the use of 'Abdullāh Yūsuf 'Alī's translation of the Qur'an and a comprehensive index.*

CHAPTER 1
The Qur'an in Medieval Bondage

THE MIND of the Muslim almost all over the world is at a discount today. There is a lag between the life as enjoined on him by the Qur'an, and the life he has devised for himself. There is a lag between the social and political institutions which the Qur'an desires him to install, and the institutions which he has set up for himself and developed in the course of history. There is a lag between the purpose of the present day Muslim and the abiding purpose of the Qur'an—the world purpose. There is, in short, a big lag between the universality of the Qur'an and the isolationist religiosity of the present-day Muslim. If one should probe the lives of those who profess to believe in other sacred books—better the task be undertaken by some ardent follower of each—we shall not be surprised if similar lags meet the eye.

In his *Ihyā' al-'Ulūm*, Ghazālī records an incident in the life of Caliph 'Umar.[1] The Caliph was travelling from Madīnah to Makkah. On the way one early morning, he noticed a flock of

---

1 Al-Ghazālī, *Ihyā' 'Ulūm al-Dīn*, Cairo: Dār al-Kutub al-'Arabiyyah al-Kubra, 1334 AH, vol. IV, p. 840.

sheep at the base of a hillock. A Negro boy was tending the flock. To test whether the teachings of the Qur'an had, at least in their elementary form, ever reached this Negro boy living in a remote corner of Arabia and to what extent he had reacted to them in his individual life, he asked him if he would like to sell one of the lambs in the flock. Promptly a definite "No" was the answer. "But why?" asked the Caliph. "Why?—Because it is not mine", rejoined the Negro boy. "It is my master's, and I am his slave". "What matters?" said the Caliph. "Take this money, give that lamb to me; and go and tell your master that some wolf snatched away his lamb". The boy stared hard at the Caliph. The poor fellow did not know whom he was staring at. "I can cheat my master over there on the other side of the hillock. But can I," he stressed, "cheat that Great Master who is overlooking both of us and listening?" The boy was an illiterate boy. He had never read the Qur'an. But the atmospheric influence of its teachings had evidently touched his mind. He must have heard in some manner the Qur'anic words that God "knows what dark suggestions his soul makes to him" and that He is "nearer to him than his jugular vein" (*Qāf*, 50:16), and that "there is no secret consultation between three, but He makes the fourth among them,—nor between five but He makes the sixth,—nor between fewer nor more, but He is in their midst wheresoever they be" (*al-Mujādilah*, 58:7). He must also have heard that none can give away or sell anything which does not belong to him. What profound impression the reply of this Negro boy must have created on the mind of a man like 'Umar, that austere and mighty Caliph of Islam, can easily be imagined. "Tears rolled down his cheeks", says the narrative. Tenderly he asked the boy to lead him on to his worldly master, the owner of the flock. On meeting him the Caliph enquired: "How much did you pay for this slave?" "So much", replied the owner. "Here is that much, take it, and set the boy free".

Of course, the boy became a free man and 'Umar went his way. But the question may as well be asked: How many of us, whether Muslim or non-Muslim, in all stations and walks of life, how many brilliant products of our Universities, how many of those who conduct today the affairs of their countries, indeed, how many of those who have subscribed to the Charter of the United Nations and the Universal Declaration of Human Rights have attained that stage of mind or attitude which this Negro boy of 1,300 years back had reached or have felt the same sense of God and held themselves responsible to Him in all that they have thought or done in their several lives?

It is this sense of God which the Qur'an aims to inspire in man, and base thereon an order of society every member of which shall be a "keeper or shepherd unto every other",[2]—a brotherhood co-extensive in its final reaches with the whole of mankind who, in the words of the Prophet of Islam, constitute the "Family of God".[3] The state of Madīnah which he shaped and passed on to the Caliphs grew at first into a democracy different fundamentally in its structure and outlook from that of the ancient Athenians, a democracy composed of individuals who conscious of the dignity of human nature recognised no criterion

---

2 *Saḥīḥ al-Bukhārī, op. cit.*, 'Kitāb al-Jumu'ah', *ḥadīth* no. 893 (vol 1, pp.267-78); *Saḥīḥ Muslim, op. cit.*, 'Kitāb al-'Imārah', *ḥadīth* no. 1829 (vol.3, p.1495).

3 See Note 1, p. vii.

of superiority between themselves except that of righteous living, and whose earnest aim was to blend harmoniously the material into the sublime or spiritual needs of human nature and vitalize life to disclose a united happiness for all mankind.

This democracy, however, did not last long. Once the state expanded beyond the Arabian frontiers, and assumed the role of an empire, the Khilāfah which had started as an elective institution soon transformed itself into a dynastic monarchy. The transition was marked by civil wars. The bone of contention was the Khilāfah; and as that office, as instituted, had its own religious function to discharge, the struggle naturally put on a religious colour. This is not the place to judge motives or apportion blame. Indeed it will be idle to do so across the vexatious centuries which intervene. But the result was a schismatic life for Islam. The tendency let loose in the time of the civil wars to drift from the anchorage of the Qur'anic ideals gathered momentum during the dynastic Khilāfah of the Ummayids and of their successors the Abbāsids and expressed itself, assisted by alien cultural strains, into the proverbial seventy-two sects of Islam. As an offshoot of this tendency and at the same time as its source of nourishment came into play the urge by over-zealous partizans to invoke, where argument failed, the very name of the Prophet, and ascribe to him utterances and actions bodied forth from their fertile imagination in support of their rival claims and standpoints. The earnest among the followers of the Faith grew alarmed at the rapidity of pace with which the stories were coined. Their task was to check this tendency and rescue the Qur'an and the picture of the Prophet from submergence. How onerous was the task may be gleaned from the fact that when Bukhārī undertook to sift the authentic from the spurious and codify what seemed to him the genuine *hadīth* or traditions of the Prophet, he had to discard, out of nearly 600,000 of which, according to Ibn Khallikan, he took cognizance,[4] all except 7397 according to some authorities or 7295 according to others, as fabrications or not worthy of credence. Indeed, if repetitions under different heads or chapters are to be discarded, the number will be reduced to 2,762.[5] The criterion applied by him was the veracity of the narrators of the *hadīth*, and not exactly the character of their contents. The idea evidently was to eliminate the professional manufacturers of *hadīth* from the canonical list. Yet, there is valid ground to hold, particularly on the basis of internal evidence, that notwithstanding the care and integrity exercised in the choice of guarantors, there are still a number of *hadīth* in the corpus of Bukhārī and of his imitators the authenticity of which needs to be endorsed, if they are to stand, by methods of scientific enquiry and research.

The *hadīth* literature is held in importance and sacredness generally next to the Qur'an and in certain circles it takes even precedence over the Qur'an.[6] It was at first intended to serve as a record of the practice of the Prophet. in relation to the commandments of the Qur'an expressed but in general terms. It was to supply clarification and to show the manner of

---

4 Ibn Khallikan: *Wafayāt al-A'yān*, ed. Wustenfeld, p. 580.

5 Alfred Guillaume: *The Traditions of Islam*, Oxford: Oxford University Press, 1924, p. 28.

6 Ibid. p. 43.

implementing them in every new situation that might arise in the life of the faithful subject always to the imperative demands of unity. But soon, as indicated above, the purpose was, under some urge or other, widened, sometimes recklessly; so much so, that within three centuries of the passing of the Prophet, this new literature gave rise to a number of entire systems of law, theology, and custom, each designated Islam, none of which, however, was precisely the Islam which the Prophet bequeathed to his people on the day of his Farewell Address at Makkah. Thus the faith of the Qur'an which called upon its followers to "hold fast by the rope of God" (*Āli 'Imrān*, 3:103), and live a united life was itself pressed into the service of a divided life by the very people who professed to believe in it.

To make matters worse, the spirit and purpose underlying the manner of presentation in the Qur'an, the style and diction, was not properly comprehended during the period when the first commentaries on the Book were undertaken—commentaries which often failed to discriminate the *muhkamāt* or verses bearing plain and clear meaning or things to be taken in the literal sense from the *mutashābihāt* and *amthāl* or similitudes, and figures of speech, between which the Qur'an expressly calls upon its readers to make proper distinction. In consequence, the very essentials of the Faith and practice came to be viewed in the light of the faiths and traditions of the races, both Arab and non-Arab, converted to Islam, from among whom the commentators sprang up, giving to the allegorical or figurative element in the Qur'an either a literal sense or a sense alien to the very spirit of the Qur'anic message. The impact is partly pagan in character reflected in the anthropomorphic touches given to the concept of

The Qur'an in Medieval Bondage

divinity and its attributes, and partly mystic in its significance as inspired essentially by Neoplatonism, and manifested chiefly in the *A'jamī* or non-Arab attempt to read esoteric meaning into, what is basically exoteric or mundane in the Qur'an. Not merely this, the sense of superiority or imperialism engendered in the minds of the Arabs by their sweeping conquests developed the tendency to give to passages in the Qur'an or *hadīth* touching usages peculiar to the Arabs or certain passing incidents in the life of the Prophet, the force of universal applicability to all times and conditions of existence. Even as in the field of *hadīth*, there is now a great need for scientific research in the field of interpretation of the Qur'anic phraseology as well, and for distinguishing between the merely incidental and the abiding directions of the Qur'an.

But the net result, the legacy of the past, such as it is, is what has to be faced today. The lines of thought laid down a thousand years ago have, in spite of reformatory attempts made every now and then to remould the Muslim mind on Qur'anic lines, vitiated the entire course of Muslim thought and history. The Qur'an is read parrot-like in most Muslim homes. It is explained in every mosque from week to week. Its language is employed in every daily prayer. But the sense of the word read, recited, or explained is not always the original Qur'anic sense. It is the sense given to it primarily in the times of the Ummayyids and the Abbāsids, in the middle ages. The religion that passes for Islam today—the Islam of the masses and of the ruling classes in every Muslim country is the Islam of the Middle Ages and not exactly the Islam of the Qur'an and the Prophet. Its outward form is there, however dishevelled, but the spirit in essential respects is un-Qur'anic. No wonder then that the mind of the present day Muslim—of course there are and must be exceptions everywhere, "the salt of the earth",—is not of the type which that poor illiterate slave Negro boy of the time of 'Umar endeavoured to represent even in the restricted sphere of his life.

No doubt Medieval Muslim History can claim with legitimate pride great advances in the realm of Arts, Sciences and Philosophy. But this achievement had no organic connection with the day to day life of the Muslim. It formed the exclusive concern of the intellectual élite and bore little relation to the social and religious life of the life of the masses who were kept down in ignorance and were simply nose-led by the reactionary 'Ulamā' or doctors of religion of the times, most of whom were stipendiaries of autocratic rulers whose political interests they had to subserve. The medieval mind has persisted to live on and in its several local variations still operative in every nook and corner of the Muslim world.

It is not my purpose to go into the history of this development, although in my discourse a passing reference here and there to its leading features or landmarks may be found necessary in the interests of clarity and emphasis. On the other hand, I shall, in the light of the Qur'an and the uncontested facts of the life of the Prophet endeavour to present, though on a limited canvas, the picture of the mind of man which his function in life warrants him to mould for himself, particularly at this hour, and face the serious complex problems confronting mankind with becoming confidence. My appeal will be to the intellect of man as man and although addressed primarily to those who claim to follow the Qur'an, is intended to rouse the mood of introspection among others as well, for, the ailment of which the Muslim has been a victim has also in one form or another held under its grip the rest of mankind as well. In the presentation of my subject, I shall, as far as possible, avoid the use of technical phraseology for the simple reason that the Qur'an itself does not use any technical terms and is meant to be intelligible even to that illiterate Negro boy tending a flock of sheep in his capacity as a slave.

CHAPTER 2
The Moorings

THE QUR'AN is essentially a code of human conduct. That is the claim which the Book itself advances (*al-Baqarah*, 2:2-5). It is meant to offer guidance to those who may be disposed to seek it. It differs from abstract ethics in this that it purports to possess a religious sanction for those who choose to follow it, and covers a wider field of activity than what is envisaged by the latter. That by itself does not divest it of its value to those who may fight shy of religion. For, however wide and deep the religious character of its background, the line of conduct delineated by the Qur'an is to be endorsed in action by a rational approach to it, and is on that account a subject for consideration even by those who may not believe in any established religion, but who nevertheless dislike anarchy in thought and action and recognise the need for some standard of conduct to govern their daily activity. To such, it may be told that the essential purpose of the Qur'an is to develop in man a mind the immediate function of which is to enable him to live in peace with himself and in peace with his external world of relations, although in so doing he is to serve a deeper purpose as well. This wider applicability, which is beyond the purview of abstract ethics or of any exclusively secular concept of life, is warranted by the notion maintained by the Qur'an that death is not the end of life, but that, on the other hand, it is a gateway to a new sphere of activity, marking a further stage in the making of man. "Ye shall surely travel from stage to stage" (*al-Inshiqāq*, 84:19) is the vista of possibilities disclosed, and the succeeding life is conditioned by the present. It is the ultimate purpose—the perfection of man—that should govern the character of life one has to live in the present. The mind which the Qur'an aims to build is therefore to view in one sweep the entire life of man, the present and what is to follow, and treat it as a single entity, and adjust its movement accordingly. "Your creation or your resurrection is in no wise but as an individual soul" (*Luqmān*, 31:28).

The building of this mind, as well as, its manifestation in every sphere of interest to the mind—the entire cultural course of the Qur'an—is summed up in but a phrase "Believe and work righteously." That is the way to develop the mind favoured of the Qur'an. 'Belief' is thus the force which lends tone or character to the mind, and work in consonance thereof is but a reflection of it in action. Let us, therefore, dwell awhile on what the mind is to be fed on, the beliefs which one has to entertain as sources of his inspiration to righteous work. This is in the nature of things necessary; for to appraise the value of the activity of a mind, it is essential to appraise at first the very character of its foundation, the factors and forces which mould it, the ingredients which enter into its composition, indeed the moorings from which it may not stray.

Unity of God

The basic concept into which the Qur'an desires to initiate the human mind is the concept of the Unity of God—a concept on which it wishes another concept, the Unity of man, to rest and receive life and sustenance therefrom. *Lā Ilāha Illallāh*: 'There is none worthy of worship except God' is the concept on which such strong stress is laid that the entire Qur'an seems to be nothing else than an exposition of its implications and a commentary of it. The late Rev. C. F. Andrews in one of his writings observes:

> "One of the greatest blessings which Islam has brought to East and West alike has been the emphasis which at a critical period in human history it placed upon the Divine Unity. For during those Dark Ages both in East and West, from 600 to 1000 AD this doctrine was in danger of being overlaid and obscured in Hinduism and in Christianity itself, owing to the imense accretions of subsidiary worships of countless demi-gods and heroes. Islam has been, both to Europe and India, in their dark hour of aberration from the sovereign truth of God's Unity, an invaluable corrective and deterrent. Indeed, without the final emphasis on this truth, which Islam gave from its central position,—facing India and facing Europe—it is doubtful whether this idea of God as one could have obtained that established place in human thought which is uncontested in the intellectual world today".[1]

Looking therefore at the low ebb to which human thought and life had descended at the time when Muḥammad was passing

---

[1] *The Genuine Islam*, Singapore, vol. I: no. 8, 1936.

from adolescence into manhood and from manhood into maturity, the voice in him that expressed itself in this formula was indeed the imperative voice of Humanity out to assert itself, and consequently was heard throughout Arabia, and even across its frontiers during his own life-time. The spiritual implications of the concept of Divine Unity will be touched upon in the later stages of this discourse, but it may be observed here that its pragmatic value to man in his social relations was immense. The idea that there was none worthy of worship except God swept off all distinctions of colour and race, and every hierarchical conception of life, social and political. It was a revolutionary slogan aiming at the emancipation of man. It restored dignity to human nature by placing man next to God and making righteous living the sole test of superiority of one over another.

Unity of Man

Alongside of stimulating in man the sense of human dignity, the Qur'an calls upon him to recognise that "mankind was but one nation", that subsequently it "differed" (*Yūnus*, 10:19) and that it should therefore be man's endeavour to restore its unity (*al-Baqarah*, 2:209).

So great is the importance attached by the Qur'an to the maintenance of the unity of man that the Prophet looks upon the entire mankind as the family of God.

"All creatures of God are His family, and he is the most beloved of God who loveth best His creatures".[2]

---

2 See note 1, p. vii.

"Respect the ways of Allah (or the laws inherent in Nature) and be affectionate to the family of Allah."

The Qur'an declares:

If any one slew a person—unless it be for murder or for spreading mischief in the land—it would be as if he slew the whole people: and if any one saved a life, it would be as if he saved the life of the whole people.

al-Mā'idah, 5:32

The idea so strongly emphasised by the Qur'an over 1,300 years ago that mankind was but one and the same species of creation and that the theory of race was a social myth operating for the disunity of man, may now be regarded as a scientific fact. Read the latest and the most authoritative statement of modern scientific doctrine on the subject of race issued by the UNESCO (July 1950). That statement sets forth the conclusions of an international panel of scientists formed by the UNESCO to define the concept of race and to summarise the most recent findings in this field which the world's biologists, geneticists, psychologists, sociologists, and anthropomologists agree are established scientific facts. The text of the statement issued by the experts opens in words reminescent of the language of the Qur'an quoted above.

"Scientists have reached the general agreement in recognizing that mankind is one, that all men belong to the same species—*Homo Sapiens*".

It concludes with the ethical implication of this fact of life covered by the saying of the Prophet:

"Every one of you is a keeper unto every other, and will be accountable for the welfare of his fold".[3]

Runs the scientists' conclusions in the following words:
"Biological studies lend support to the ethic of universal brotherhood; for man is born with drives toward cooperation, and unless these drives are satisfied, men and nations alike fall ill. Man is born a social being who can reach his fullest development only through interaction with his fellows. The denial at any point of this social bond between man and man brings with it disintegration. In this sense, every man is his brother's keeper. For every man is a piece of the continent, a part of the main, because he is involved in mankind".

The Unity of man receiving its sustenance from the Unity of God is in its social bearing the leading theme of the Qur'an. To promote that unity, the Qur'an calls upon man first to develop the sense of catholicity in life. Religion was one of the important fields—probably the most important in the days of the Prophet—where conflict thrived. The Qur'an first aimed at the elimination of this conflict. Christianity and Judaism were the religions which prevailed at the time in the Semetic sector. The Qur'an desires the Prophet to negotiate a *modus vivendi* with the followers of the two faiths.

Say: "O People of the Book! come to common terms as between as and you: that we worship none but God; that we associate no partners with Him; that we erect not, from

---

[3] *Sahīh al-Bukhārī*, 'Kitāb al-Ahkām', no. 7138, vol.4, p.444.

among ourselves, lords and patrons other than God."
'Āli 'Imrān, 3:64

The condition of association advanced here is that God alone is to be the Lord, and none else. The privilege is not to be confined to one's relations with Christians or Jews alone. It extends to the followers of all other religions, provided the basic condition is fulfilled—belief in the Unity of God. That such a belief is the basis of all religions is repeatedly asserted by the Qur'an, and that in consequence they should not work in antagonism with one another, but work conjointly for world unity. Addressing the Prophet, the Qur'an says:

> *The same religion has He established for you as that which He enjoined on Noah—that which We have sent by inspiration to thee—and that which We enjoined on Abraham, Moses, and Jesus: namely, that ye should remain steadfast in Religion, and make no divisions therein.*
> *al-Shūrā*, 42:13

> *Verily We have sent thee in truth, as a bearer of glad tidings, and as a warner: and there never was a people without a warner having lived among them.*
> *Fāṭir*, 35:24

> *We did aforetime send messengers before thee: of them there are some whose story We have related to thee, and some whose story We have not related to thee.*
> *Ghāfir*, 40:78

The Qur'an sums up:
> *Say: "We believe in God, and in what has been revealed to us and what was revealed to Abraham, Ismā'īl, Isaac, Jacob, and the Trives, and in (the Books) given to Moses, Jesus and the prophets, from their Lord: we make no distinction between one and another among them, and to God do we bow our will (in Islam)".*
> *Āli 'Imrān*, 3:84

> *And verily this Brotherhood of yours is a single Brotherhood.*
> *al-Mu'minūn*, 23:52

In building up this catholicity of mind, the Qur'an is careful enough not to let the Arabic speaking people feel that the Arabic language in which the Qur'anic Message is delivered is by any means exclusively sacrosanct or is the exclusive language of God. God expresses Himself in all tongues.

> *We sent not a messenger except (to teach) in the language of his (own) people, in order to make (things) clear to them.*
> *Ibrāhīm*, 14:4

So wide is the catholic attitude of mind intended to be simulated that the Qur'an promises salvation not merely to the people of the Qur'an but to those also among whom other scriptures have been delivered—not merely to these, but to every human being not believing in any established church but who nevertheless acknowledges the value of Divine unity in human life and recognises responsibility for his actions, and lives uprightly.

> *Those who believe (in the Qur'an) and those who follow the Jewish (scripture), and the Christians and the Sabians,—any who believe in God and the Last Day, and work righteousness, shall have their reward with their Lod; on them shall be no fear, nor shall they grieve.*
> al-Baqarah, 2:62

The privilege extends even to those who are not attached to any established faith.

> *Verily those who say, "Our Lord is God", and remain firm (on that Path),—on them shall be no fear, nor shall they grieve. Such shall be Companions of the Garders, dwelling therein (for aye): a recompense for their (good) deeds.*
> al-Aḥqāf, 46:13-14

The idea underlying this catholic attitude was to eliminate friction between the followers of the different faiths and rest their relationship on a common belief in the unity of God consciously operating for the unity of man.

> *O mankind! We created you from a single (pair) of a male and a female, and made you into nations and tribes, that ye may know each other (not that ye may despise each other). Verily the most honoured of you in the sight of God is (he who is) the most righteous of you. And God has full knowledge and is well-acquainted (with all things).*
> al-Ḥujurāt, 49:13

Mark the phrase "care for each other". That was, under the

The Moorings

plan of the Prophet, the common ground on which all humanity can and should enter to work together for their common good and live as a "family of God". That is the way to an abiding fraternal relationship between man and man. The world order on which the Prophet set his heart was to be composed of not merely those who would follow the Qur'an in every detail, but all others who in common would believe in the Unity of God and righteous living in accordance therewith. His supreme insistence on this minimum, a belief in the unity of God inspiring righteous living in man, was for no other reason than to let that sense of divine Unity transform itself into the sense of the unity of man. It is in this context that the term *kufr* plays such an important part in the Qur'anic thought. The term has acquired an odium among non-Muslim circles purely through its incorrect grasp by the medieval commentators of the Qur'an and its indiscriminate and reckless application by fanatics to all non-Muslims and even to Muslims who differ from them in any respect. For that, the Qur'an is not responsible.

A *kāfir* in reality is one who disregards the unity of God by his thought and action and thereby becomes a force for disunity among men, which in the Qur'anic concept is a denial in practice of Divine unity. The Qur'an therefore makes no compromise with *kufr*, for, it is obvious that *kufr*, the force for disunity, cannot co-exist, much less work hand in hand with the force for unity in any conceivable scheme of things aiming at the unity of man. Barring this ideological difference with *kufr* in all its forms and wherever found, in other words, with all forces of disintegration or disunity, the basic attitude of the Qur'an towards other faiths is either of seeking a *modus vivendi* as already indicated or of tacit tolerance and forbearance in the earnest hope and trust that one day "God will bring them all together" and advance the cause of divine unity working itself out in the unity of man.

> *Now then, for that (reason), call (them to the Faith), and stand steadfast as thou art commanded, nor follow thou their vain desires; but say: "I believe in the Book which God has sent down; and I am commanded to judge justly between you. God is our Lord and your Lord: for us (is the responsibility for) our deeds, and for you for your deeds. There is no contention between us and you. God will bring us together, and to Him is (our) final goal".*
>
> al-Shūrā, 42:15

The unity of man thus is one of the main objectives man has to pursue in life through a programme of righteous work—work in consonance with his belief in the unity of God, and points to the role he has to play in life.

The Role of Man

As we have already pointed out, the leading idea of the Qur'an *Lā Ilāha Illallāh*; 'there is none worthy of worship except God', determines man's place in the scheme of creation. It does not relegate him to a position of inferiority to any object of creation. He is not inferior in stature in the scale of Divine values to the Sun or the Moon or other constellations in the heavens which have formed the objects of worship from a distance in the history of man, or to anything in the earth at close range, or again to that body of invisible forces at work in nature styled *malā'ikah* or

Angels. The Qur'an points out that man is made "in the best of moulds" (*al-Tīn*, 95:4), he whom the *malā'ikah* were made to offer obeisance and for whom whatsoever is in the heavens and whatsoever is in the earth are made to do service (*Luqmān*, 31:20).

Thus raised in the scale of creation and placed immediately next to God, man's importance is further emphasised by investing him with the privilege of living on Earth as the vicegerent of God Himself.

The truth is brought home in figurative language the phraseology of which brings to mind the striking lines of Matthew Arnold entitled "Revolutions":

"Before man parted for this earthly strand,
While yet upon the verge of heaven he stood,
God put a heap of letters in his hand,
And bade him make with them what word he could
And man has turned them many times: made Greece,
Rome, England, France:— Yes, nor in vain essayed
Way after way, changes that never cease.
The letters have combined: something was made."

Indeed, something was made; but the poet in sorrow exclaims:

"Ah; an inextinguishable sense
Haunts him that he has not made what he should,
That he has still, though old, to recommence,
Since he has not yet found the word God would.
And empire after empire, at their height
Of sway, have felt this boding sense come on;
Have felt their huge frames not constructed right,
And dropped, and slowly died upon their throne."

That was Arnold's approach, evidently inspired by St John's: 'In the beginning was the Word and the Word was with God, and the Word was God'. Here the purpose of man was to find out that Word. On the other hand, the reflex process is what is revealed by the Qur'an. It does not suggest that God merely 'put a heap of letters into man's hand when he parted for this earthly strand and bade him to make with them what word he could'. It affirms that the 'Word' itself was shown to him and its meaning explained, and lest he might forget its structure and composition was transfixed in his nature, bidding him to preserve it therein and not to play with its letters and disturb their arrangement, so that he might live in peace with himself and in peace with his external world of relations.

> *Behold, thy Lord said to the angels: "I will create a vicegerent on earth". They said: "Wilt Thou place therein one who will make mischief therein and shed blood?—whilst we do celebrate Thy praises and glorify Thy holy (name)?" He said: "I know what ye know not".*
>
> *And He taught Adam the nature of all things; then He placed them before the angels, and said: "Tell me the nature of these if ye are right".*
>
> *They said: "Glory to Thee, of knowledge we have none, save what Thou hast taught us: in truth it is Thou Who art perfect in knowledge and wisdom.*
>
> *He said: "O Adam! tell them their natures". When he had told them, God said: "Did I not tell you that I know the secrets of heaven and earth, and I know what ye reveal and what ye conceal?"*
>
> *al-Baqarah, 2:30-33*

Thus rendered conscious of the purpose of creation and of the 'names' or the meaning of things, or the laws of their existence, it followed as a corollary that man should affirm the unity of existence.

> *When thy Lord drew forth from the Children of Adam—from their loins—their descendants, and made them testify concerning themselves, (saying): "Am I not your Lord?"—They said: "Yea, we do testify!"*
>
> al-A'rāf, 7:172

So equipped, man's nature found itself agreeable to bear the trust of vicegerency.

> *We did indeed offer the Trust to the Heavens and the Earth and the Mountains; but they refused to undertake it, being afraid thereof: but man undertook it.*
>
> al-Ahzāb, 33:72

The undertaking was on the face of it, not an easy affair. The Qur'an is struck by its very audacity as the continuation of the verse suggests:

> *He was indeed unjust and foolish.*

But the purpose of his creation was nevertheless to carry him "from stage to stage" (*al-Inshiqāq*, 84:19) toward perfection. The process was designed for him as part of the divine scheme—an aspect of creative evolution to which fuller attention will be drawn in due course. But to lessen the pang implicit in the ordeal and to help man bear the trust undertaken, and to keep the life intended for him or the letters of the 'Word' revealed to him in proper form, says the Qur'an, a sense of balance was set in his nature and he was told that he would be judged according to the use he makes of it.

> *By the Soul and proportion and order given to it. And its enlightenment as to its wrong and its right. Truly he succeeds that purifies it. And he fails that corrupts it.*
>
> al-Shams, 91:7-10

The truth of the last verse is expressed by the Qur'an in a paradox, each side of which is meant to be equally true:

> *We have indeed created man in the best of moulds. Then do we debase him (to be) the lowest of the low.*
>
> al-Tīn, 95:4-5

Every thinker in every age has had to recognise this paradox in human nature. The task of every religion has been to save man from sinking in the scale of life. Says the Qur'an in continuation of the paradox for the sake of clearing the issue raised therein:

> *Then do we abase him (to be) the lowest of the low, except such as believe and do righteous deeds.*
>
> al-Tīn, 95:5-6

Some lay stress on faith or belief as the means of salvation. But 'belief' alone is not enough in Islam. "Righteous work in consonance therewith" is equally necessary. That is the way to preserve his goodliest fabric and help him discharge his responsibility as the vicegerent of God on earth. This vicegerency, as often proclaimed in the history of man, is not the

The Moorings

divine right of churches or of kings to govern men as they liked. On the other hand it is the inherent right of mankind to govern themselves and regulate their lives in conformity with the principle of order and harmony noticeable in divine creation:

So set thou thy face steadily and truly to the Faith: (establish) God's handiwork according to the pattern on which He has made mankind: no change (let there be) in the work (wrought) by God: that is the standard Religion: but most among mankind understand not.

al-Rūm, 30:30

It is those who respect the ways of God and scrupulously follow them in life who alone are to be truly regarded as the vicegerents of God on earth. Their function is to be interpreted in terms of the good that they can offer not only to themselves and to fellowmen, but to all living objects on earth who form together in the words of the Prophet "the family of God", every one of whom has a being from their Maker "and to whom they will be gathered".

There is not an animal (that lives) on the earth, nor a being that flies on its wings, but (forms part of) communities like you. Nothing have We omitted from the Book, and they (all) shall be gathered to their Lord in the end.

al-An'ām, 6:38

The function of man in his role as the Vicegerent of God on earth is to be discharged not merely to let him live in peace with himself and in peace with the external world of relations, but is to be pursued with an eye on what is called the "Life hereafter".

"Unto their Lord will all be gathered" is the prospect which the Qur'an holds out to every one, before Whom every one will have to tender an account of what he or she had done during his or her present life. The idea of a "return to God" has thus been raised by the Qur'an to the position of a cardinal belief for man and is as important to his life as the belief in the unity of God expressing itself in the unity of man through a programme of righteous work or *'amal sālih*.

CHAPTER 3
The Equipment

HOW IS the task to be performed? The answer is summed up in a single word—Islam or "devotion to *sunnat Allāh* or the ways of Allah", for which, according to the Qur'an, "the pattern on which He has made mankind" (*al-Rūm*, 30:30). In a lucid exposition of this term, as in essence common to all established faiths, Dr J. H. Bridges, a positivist, follower of Comte, observes in a discourse delivered as far back as 1879:

> "The faith of the Mussalman is concentrated in a single word, Islam, devotion, resignation of our own will to the Supreme decree. That word was not limited by Mohammad to his own followers; it was used ungrudgingly of his Judaic and Christian predecessors. There is no fitter word for the religion of the human race. If there is any one word in western language which can translate it fully, it is the word 'religion' itself; and that word needs interpretation for ears untrained in Latin speech. The word Islam unfolds itself for us, as for the followers of Mohammad, into the two great and inseparable aspects of life—prayer and work. 'Pray and give alms,' said Mohammad, alms-giving in his wide interpretation of it, conceived with admirable wisdom relatively to the simple wants of his time, covering the whole field of doing good to men. 'Pray and work,' said the medieval saint; pray as though nothing were to be done by work: work as though

nothing ware to be gained by prayer.

In different ways and under every possible variety of language and symbol, the same thing is said by every spiritual leader of men in every age and country. I find it in Confucius, the founder of the faith that has kept Chinese Society together for five-and-twenty centuries: I find it in the ancient theocracy of Hindostan: I find it in the monuments of Egypt as their secrets are gradually revealing themselves to modern learning: I read it in the premature effort of Pythagoras, premature, yet profoundly fruitful of momentous result to discipline of life upon a human basis: and last of all, I find it where most men think a monopoly of such knowledge is to be found, in the Hebrew and Christian Bible.

Islam, then, or in the, English tongue, devotion—the devotion of our life to the highest; the bringing of our own will into accord with the supreme will; this is the word that sums up the lives of pious men in every age and every country. They have framed for themselves an ideal, a model, a pattern of what their life should be. They have done their utmost to make that ideal a reality. In other words, they have prayed, and they have worked."[1]

How then is one to bring one's own will into accord with the Supreme Will? The task is two-fold. It consists in the first place, of faith or belief; and in the second, of work in consonance therewith. It is not merely 'Pray and Work', which constitutes the function of man. On the other hand, the Qur'anic commandment is 'Believe and Work righteously'. Prayer in Islam is more an action of the spirit and is covered by the term 'work'. The Qur'an emphasises that belief by itself is not enough. Indeed

---

[1] J. H. Bridges: *Discourses on Positive Religion*, London: Reaves and Turner, 1891, pp. 3-4.

belief without work appropriate to it is static. Mere philosophic perception of the essence of divinity or contemplation is barren, if it does not generate volition or give movement to human life in consonance with the qualities or attributes of that essence. Mere spiritual exercises of the kind which certain religious orders practice, or psychic achievements, however interesting, will not rise above their character as but the exercises of the mind, if they do not contribute to and subserve a dynamic moral existence for man. This dynamic morality again is not possible for one who seeks his individual spiritual salvation through the life of the cloister or the cave, or for one who through abnegation of his body fancies his duty to lie in merely nursing his soul. The vicegerency of God on earth is not possible for such. On the other hand, it is for him who imbues himself with divine attributes to the best of his ability and manifests them harmoniously in devoted service to himself and his fellow beings.

The attributes of God are various, as are His 'names'. They cannot be numbered, since the fullest comprehension of Divine activity is scarcely possible for man circumscribed as he is by the nature of his being. In the words of the Qur'an, "to God alone belong all excellent names" (*al-A'rāf*, 7:180) for perfection is His only in everything that He attributeth to Himself. With this general attitude towards the conception of Divine attributes, the task before man is to understand the significance to his life of such of them as are specifically brought to mind in the Qur'an. Some of these may come essentially within the purview of mysticism. But a large majority of them suggestive of His knowledge, and power, and justice, and mercy, and His tender concern for the moral purification of man may easily form the subject of social study. Even these make an imposing list, and should lay bare the futility of encasing the Divine Being in any single virtue or attribute, and incarnating Him. God in Islam is above every attribute and manifests them all in harmonious relation with one another. Man's role is to imitate God in His attributes to the extent his nature helps him.

The persistent call of the Qur'an to man is to ponder on the working of the external world of creation. Therein is at work, it suggests, the eternal principle of harmony and balance to urge on man the need for devoted imitation:

*The Sun and the Moon follow courses (exactly) computed,
And the herbs and the trees—both (alike) bow in adoration
And the Firmament has He raised high, and He has set up the Balance (of Justice),
In order that ye may not transgress (due) balance.
So establish weight with justice and fall not short in the balance*

al-Rahmān, 55:5-9

He Who created the seven heavens one above another : no want of proportion wilt thou see in the Creation of (God) Most Gracious. So turn thy vision again: seest thou any flaw? Again turn thy vision a second time: (thy) vision will come back to thee dull and discomfited, in a state worn out.

al-Mulk, 67:3-4

The essential task of man therefore who aspires to rise in the scale of life and play the role of a vicegerent of God on Earth is to work for harmony not merely in his own life but in that of the

The Equipment

world surrounding him. The injunction "Believe and work righteously" has therefore different meanings for the different stages in the scale of life to which man has to rise from step to step to qualify himself for his task in high and higher spheres of activity. Those who undertake this great journey in life in the light of the Qur'anic directions are not all grouped together under a single category. The Qur'an speaks of several types of travellers traversing the path of Allah, according to the divine attributes they display in their onward march. It gives each type a distinct name. They are to be known by their action; by their work and not by their mere belief. In fact not every one who says he believes in Islam is included in the ranks of the '*Mu'minīn*' or 'Believers' unless his belief is endorsed by appropriate action. These types are severally addressed as *sālihīn, muttaqīn, muslihīn, muflihīn, muqsitīn, sābirīn, shākirīn, muhsinīn, sādiqīn, siddīqīn, shuhadā', awliyā', muslimīn, muqarribīn, ūlu'l-'ilm, ūlu'l-albāb*, and so on. But this is to be observed that one common purpose binds them all, the essential purpose of displaying in their lives the 'balance and harmony' dwelling in the Divine scheme of things.

As against this order favoured of the Qur'an, there stands the opposite order of those upon whom the Qur'an looks with distinct disfavour. They are of those who disturb the 'Balance and harmony' that should subsist in life, and 'create mischief in the earth'. They too are classified by the quality of the evil they display in their activity, designated as *kāfirīn, mushrikīn, zalimīn, mufsidīn, ghāfilīn, munāfiqīn* and so forth.

The types of people favoured of the Qur'an, are by no means exclusive types. They are classified differently simply on the basis of the divine attribute each displays in its activity more noticeably than any other. Indeed, the larger the number of attributes one displays more or less in equal measure, the higher his station in life and the greater his capacity to discharge his responsibilities as the vicegerent of God on Earth.

It is He Who hath made you (His) agents, inheritors of the earth: He hath raised you in ranks, some above others: that He may try you in the gifts He hath given you.

al-An'ām, 6:165

Of all the divine attributes with which man has to endue himself for his task, knowledge commands precedence. Its acquisition is a duty on every man and every woman as laid by the Prophet of Islam:

"Acquire knowledge," said he, "It enables the possessor to distinguish right from wrong. It lights the way to heaven; it is our companion when friendless, it guides us to happiness and sustains us in adversity. It is a weapon against enemies and an ornament among friends. By virtue of it, Allah exalteth nations, and maketh them guides in good pursuits, and giveth them leadership; so much so, that their footsteps are followed, their deeds are imitated, and their opinions are accepted and, held in respect".[2]

The *ūlu'l-'ilm* (those who equip themselves with knowledge or the learned) naturally deserve our primary attention. For, knowledge is the means whereby the qualities, characteristic of

---

2 Editor's note: The author has liberally quoted the ḥadīth. See it in full in Abū 'Umar Yūsuf: *Jāmi' al-Bayān al-'Ilm wa Faḍlih*, Beirut: Dār al-Kutub al-'Ilmiyyah, n.d., vol. 1, pp. 54-55.

the other types, are cultivated.

There is no god but He: that is the witness of God, His angels, and those endued with knowledge, standing firm on justice.

Āli 'Imrān, 3:18

Such is the value the Qur'an sets on learning. The qualities for instance of *tawwābīn* (those who level up their path by removing all ruggedness therefrom), *sālihīn* (those who follow the right path), *muslihīn* (those who set things right), *muhsinīn* (those who do good deeds in a manner calculated to stimulate the thought of good deeds in others and help them to rectify their errors and do good deeds), *muflihīn* (those who reform or improve the condition of society) *muqsitīn* (those who admit the right of every one else and practice equity, and not merely give freedom of action to those who wish to do good deeds, but also help them in so doing), and *siddīqīn* (those who meticulously adhere to fact and truth), *muslimīn* (those who conform their will to the Will of God or submit)—the qualities distinguishing these and other types are not possible to develop except for one who is endowed with knowledge. Hence it is that the Prophet of Islam lays its acquisition as a primary duty on every man and woman and calls upon the seeker to go to the ends of the Earth in its pursuit, even to China, the then known remotest corner of the world.[3]

---

3 *Mishkāt, 'Kitāb al-'Ilm'*. Editor's note: The authenticity of this *hadīth* has been widely disputed by Muslim scholars of traditions. See details in Ibn 'Adī: *al-Kāmil fī al-Du'afā*, Beirut: Dār al-Fikr, 1988, Vol. I, p.177 and Vol. 4, p.118; al-'Ajlūnī: *op. cit.*, Vol. I, p.154, *hadīth* no. 397; al-Albānī, Muhammad

But one thing the Qur'an makes perfectly clear. Knowledge does not consist in the mere assemblage in one's memory of ideas or material on this or that subject. That does not constitute acquisition. The Qur'an desires correlation and synthesis helpful to a harmonious grasp of the verities underlying them. The Book therefore insists on reflection as an indispensable aid to the proper acquisition of knowledge.

We created not the heavens, the earth, and all between them, merely in (idle) sport. We created them not except for just ends: but most of them do not understand.

al-Dukhān, 44:38-39

"But most of them do not understand" is the regretful note that it strikes at every turn. Wherever attention is drawn to the manifestation of life calling for reflection and introspection, expressions such as "herein are portents", "herein are signs for folk who reflect", "for men of knowledge", "for folk who heed", and "for folk who understand" echo and reverberate only to emphasise the importance which the Qur'an attaches to reflection as a means of obtaining insight. "Show us the nature of things as they really are" is a characteristic prayer of the Prophet. The first step on the road to it is reflection.

Knowledge in the Qur'anic conception covers every field of life—the life of the vast universe working around man in immediate contact as well as remote, and the life of man himself moving onward with a knowledge of his past. An acquisition of

---

N.: *Silsilat al-Ahādīth al-Ḍa'īfah*, Beirut: al-Maktab al-Islāmī, 1398 H., Vol I, p. 413, *hadīth* no. 416.

knowledge therefore imposes on him the exercise of not merely his intellectual and physical faculties, but his spiritual: and nothing is prohibited to him in Islam except, probably, probing vainly the veil beyond which his reason or intuition has been found incapable of advance. And herein lies the fundamental distinction between the Qur'anic and the classic Greek culture which forms the essential basis of the modern European civilization. For, while the Greek mind reverted its attention on 'Mankind' alone or on the study of man as man, the Qur'anic mind has to take in its sweep the entire Universe, not merely the world of man, and of his spirit, but the worlds of plants, birds, animals, insects, planets, the worlds seen and the unseen—all interlinked in its consciousness, with each other, and understand and reflect on the laws underlying each creation and grasp the supreme spiritual principle of their linkage so as to fit properly into their unified existence:

> "The main purpose of the Qur'an," [points out Sir Muḥammad Iqbāl], "is to awaken in man the higher consciousness of his manifold relations with God and the universe. It is in view of this essential aspect of the Qur'anic teaching that Goethe, while making a general review of Islam as an educational force, said to Eckermann: 'You see this teaching never fails. With all our systems, we cannot go; and generally speaking no man can go, further than that.' The problem of Islam was really suggested by the mutual conflict, and at the same time mutual attraction, presented by the two forces of religion and civilization. The same problem confronted early Christianity. The great point in Christianity is the search for an independent content for spiritual life which, according to the insight of its founder, could be

elevated, not by the forces of a world external to the soul of man, but by the revelation of a world within his soul. Islam fully agrees with this insight but adds that the illumination of the new world thus revealed is not something foreign to the world of matter but permeates it through and through."[4]

The Qur'an gives man full sanction to harness the forces at work both in him and in his external world, the forces of nature, through an appropriate study of them. But it makes one condition. It calls upon man to bear in mind the balance set in his nature, and to exercise the power acquired through knowledge to help him display in his life such other attributes of God as will equip him to "show affection to the family of God" for which he has been created with the privilege of representing Him on earth by "being a shephard or keeper unto every other". If we may so express, the impersonal power of Nature that Science brings into play is to be given a personality and made conscious of the balance set therein, as in the rest of creation. In other words, it is to be humanised, and "the spirit of God breathed" into it, to use a phrase of the Qur'an. This is the primary function of human activity and is to be kept in mind in order to appraise the full import of the injunction which sums up all that is required of man: "Believe and work righteously" informed by knowledge. The wider and deeper this knowledge of one's own self and one's external world of relations, the greater the chance one has to enter the order of the *ṣāliḥīn, muttaqīn, ṣiddīqīn, muqarrabīn* and the rest who in one capacity or another fulfil the role of the

---

[4] Sir Muḥammad Iqbāl: *The Reconstruction of Religious Thought in Islam*, Oxford: Oxford University Press, 1938, p. 8.

vicegerency of God on earth.

The last named type—the *muqarrabīn*—those whom God draws to Himself—are those who aspire, in the language of the Prophet's prayer, to the knowledge of the 'Nature of things as they really are'. This knowledge of Reality the fountain-head of life, is to be gained through what is termed in the language of 'sūfīs' as *qurb ilāhī*, 'nearness to God' or 'attendance on God', loosely rendered into English as 'mystic experience', an acquisitive quality more freely developed in certain temperaments or minds spiritually inclined than in those particularly obsessed with the temporal aspects of life.

And your Lord says: "Call on Me; I will answer your (prayer).

Ghāfir, 40:60

When my servants ask thee concerning Me, I am indeed close (to them): I listen to the prayer of every suppliant when he calleth on Me.

al-Baqarah, 2:186

Here is a call for a conscious effort, and the response is immediate. Action and reaction here are synchronous. Call God in the name of His attributes and they instil themselves in you and become yours: Call Him in the name of the totality of His attributes and in the name of His essence, which clinches them all in a single unity, and you are touched by that essence and permeated through and through with it. This is the state of *qurb ilāhi*, or nearness to God or mystic experience. This mystic experience is a search for Reality and while, on the one hand, it is a form of prayer, on the other, it forms a department of knowledge, even as any other region of human experience. But the medium of knowledge is not the intellect of man but what the Qur'an calls the *qalb* or 'heart'.

"The Ṣūfī's Book," says Rūmī in describing the mystic quest after Reality, "is not composed of ink and letters: it is naught but a heart white as snow. The scholar's possession is penmarks. What is the Ṣūfī's possession?—footmarks. The Ṣūfī stalks the game like a hunter: he sees the musk deer's tract and follows the footprints. For some while the track of the deer is the proper clue for him, but afterwards it is the musk-gland of the deer that is his guide. To go one stage guided by the scent of the musk-gland is better than a hundred stages of following the track and roaming about".[5]

'Following the scent' or as the Qur'an calls 'reflection' is the first step in the mystic march to Reality.

Al-Ghazālī, himself a notable mystic, traces the process:
"Prayers have three veils, whereof the first is prayers uttered only by the tongue; the second is when the mind by hard endeavour and by firmest resolve, reaches a point at which, being untroubled by evil suggestions, it is able to concentrate itself on divine matters; the third veil is when the mind can with difficulty be diverted from dwelling on divine matters. But the marrow of prayer is seen when He who is invoked by prayer takes possession of the mind of him who prays, and the mind of the latter is absorbed in God whom he addresses, his prayers ceasing and no self-consciousness abiding in him, even to this extent that a mere thought about his prayers appear to him a veil and a hindrance. This state is called

---

5 Iqbal: *op. cit.*, p.86

'absorption' by the doctors of mystical lore, when a man is so utterly absorbed that he perceives nothing of his bodily members, nothing of what is passing without, nothing of what occurs to his mind—yea, when he is, as it were, absent things whatsoever, journeying first *to* his Lord, then *in* his Lord. But if the thought occurs to him he is totally absorbed, that is a blot; for only that absorption is worthy of the name which is unconscious of absorption. The beginning of the path is the journey to God, and that the journey in God is its goal, for in this latter, absorption in God takes place. At the outset this glides by like a flash of light barely striking the eye; but thereafter becoming habitual, it lifts the mind into a higher world, wherein the most pure, essential Reality is manifested, and the human mind is imbued with the form of the spiritual world whilst the majesty of the Deity evolves and discloses itself".[6]

The mystic experience is by its very nature incommunicable. It is intensely direct. But it can transmute itself into an idea. This is the function of mysticism or *qurb ilāhi*. Ordinarily this experience is no more than a mere sense of the unity of existence one feels,

A sense sublime of something far more deeply interfused
Whose dwelling is the light of setting suns,
And the round ocean and the living air,
And the blue sky, and in the mind of man,
A motion and a spirit that impels
All thinking things, all objects of all thought,

---

6 Jami, *Lawaih*, Oriental Translation Fund, New Series, vol. XIV—Appendix III, pp. 70-71, Royal Asiatic Society, London, 1906.

And rolls through all things.[7] —*Tintern Abbey*

Sometimes this sense strikes a deeper note and develops into a mood, that 'blessed mood',
> In which the burthen of the mystery,
> In which the heavy and the weary weight
> Of all this unintelligible world,
> Is lightened,—that serene and blessed mood,
> In which the affections gently lead us on,
> Until, the breath of this corporeal frame
> And even the motion of our human blood
> Almost suspended, we are laid asleep
> In body, and become a living soul;
> While with an eye made quiet by the power
> Of harmony, and the deep power of joy,
> We see into the life of things.[8] —*Tintern Abbey*

It is only such a mood, when it becomes habitual, at marks the beginning of what al-Ghazālī styles as the 'journey to God'. Between this stage and the beginning of the 'journey in God' there are diverse milestones to reach and pass by. The climax is 'absorption'. The history of Islam can claim countless earnest men and women who having undertaken this journey to God and thence onward in God have disdained to trace back their steps to the temporal world of man. In their several degrees, they have certainly enriched their individual lives with a vision of the

---

7 *The Poetical Works of William Wordsworth*, Edinburg, 1882, vol. I, p. 269.

8 Ibid, p. 267.

Reality; but have been lost to society. They have failed to heed the 'balance set in their nature'. Such are styled the *majdhūb* or the absorbed. They are not the type who can function, in the Qur'anic sense, as the 'vicegerents of God on earth'.

On the other hand, there have been quite a galaxy of spiritual stalwarts in Islamic history who mindful of their duty to man have come back to man, and brought with them what knowledge was vouchsafed to them in their mystic journey and spread it among mankind. The supreme example was set by the Prophet who transmuted the closest vision he had of Reality on the night of his spiritual ascent, described in chapter 53 of the Qur'an, into a plan of a new world order. On that occasion, says the Qur'an:

> *So did (God) convey the inspiration to His Servant— (conveyed) what He (meant) to convey. The (Prophet's) (mind and) heart in no way falsified that which he saw.*
> *al-Najm*, 53:10-11
>
> *(His) sight never swerved, nor did it go wrong! For truly did he see, of the Signs of his Lord, the Greatest!*
> *al-Najm*, 53:17-18

To the Prophet this was not just a vision. It had a meaning. The vision was to transmute itself into an idea of a world order, 'The family of God', every member of which was to be a shepherd unto every other.

Mystic experience, however incommunicable, has in the concept of the Qur'an its own function to discharge as a dynamic source of knowledge stimulating action worthy of the role man has to play as the vicegerent of God on Earth.

CHAPTER 4
The Will of God

'BELIEVE AND work righteously' is the comprehensive Qur'anic injunction—work, informed by knowledge.
> *For those who believe and work righteousness, is (every) blessedness, and a beautiful place of (final) return.*
> *al-Ra'd*, 13:29

But is man free to will and free to work? Expressions confront us at every turn in the Qur'an proclaiming that nothing happens except as God wills. And yet responsibility is attached to man's action: and hopes of reward and fears of punishment are held out. And then, as against this, stand out a host of verses calling upon man to exert his mind and choose between right and wrong; and he is told:
> *Verily never will God change the condition of a people until they change it themselves (with their own souls).*
> *al-Ra'd*, 13:11

> *Man can have nothing but what he strives for.*
> *al-Najm*, 53:39

> *Whatever misfortune happens to you, is because on the*

things your hands have wrought, and for many (of them) He grants forgiveness.

al-Shūrā, 42:30

What is one to make of these apparent contrarieties crossing and recrossing each other? Is man after all free to will and act or not free at all: Is there a way out? Such were the questionings which in the early centuries of Islam divided the Islamic society broadly into two warring camps—one called *qadariyyah* or those who believed in the freedom of will, and the other *Jabriyyah* or those who believed in pre-determination or absolute divine control and direction of human action.

Although this controversy reached its climax in the days of the Abbāsids, the doctrine of pre-determination had already received during the preceding Ummayyid *Khilāfah* such firm fixity in the Muslim religious thought that no other view had, in the circumstances of the times, the slightest chance to dislodge it.

At best it could be disturbed as was done under the impact of foreign strains; but it could not be supplanted. The determinist outlook not merely triumphed in the conflict, but has ever since clung to the Muslim mind and robbed the Qur'an of the corrective it had offered to this aeons' old notion prevailing in some form or other in the East. No wonder then that non-Muslim European critics have at times delivered sweeping judgements on Islam. They have called the creed of the Qur'an "devoid of love", and its God a "Pitiless tyrant, a tremendous autocrat, an uncontrolled and unsympathising Power". Take a few instances.

Says Palgrave:

"No superiority, no distinction, no pre-eminence can be lawfully claimed in Islam by one creature over another in the utter equalisation of their unexceptional servitude and abasement. All are alike tools of one solitary Force, which employs them to crush or to benefit, to truth or error, to honour or shame, to happiness or misery, quite independently of their individual fitness, deserts or advantage and simply because He wills it and as He wills it".[1]

Observes Sir William Muir:

"In Islam the relation of Allah to the world is such that not only all free will but all freedom in the exercise of the intellect is preposterous. God is so great and the character of His greatness is so pantheistically absolute that there is no room for the human. All good and all evil come directly from Allah... Hope perishes under the weight of His iron bondage and pessimism becomes the popular philosophy".[2]

Says Clarke:

"Islam saw God but not man; saw the claims of Deity, but not the rights of humanity; saw authority but failed to see freedom, therefore hardend into despotism stiffened into formalism, sank into death".[3]

Criticism of the Qur'an of the type disclosed here may be unpalatable to a Muslim, but he has to thank himself for it. The initial responsibility for it belongs to the doctors of Muslim

---

[1] W. G. Palgrave: *Narrative of a Year's Journey through Central and Eastern Arabia*, vol . I, p. 866.

[2] Quoted by S. N. Wadia in *The Message of Mohammed*, London and Toronto: Dent & Sons Ltd., 1923, p. 44.

[3] Ibid. p. 44.

theology in the Middle Ages and to their successors as well, who through an inept approach to the Qur'anic concept of the 'Will of God'—the abiding basis for right human activity—have kept the meaning and purpose of the Qur'an concealed from the mind of man giving thereby a handle to willful critics to read rank fatalism in Islam. Sir William Muir and the other writers quoted above would not go behind the interpretation of the medieval Muslim theologians on whom they depended entirely for the meaning of the Qur'an and make a direct approach to the Qur'an and apply the 'scientific method' to ascertain from the Qur'an itself what its terms such as the 'Will of God' and 'Divine Decrees' actually meant. Indeed, they could have turned to the life of the Prophet himself and sought an answer, as another student of the subject, Prof. Ardaser Sorabjee N. Wadia, a Zoroastrian by faith, tried to do in his *Message of Mohammed*. Dealing with the charge of fatalism against Islam, the Professor observes:

> "If it were so, it is obvious that nowhere would we, or ought we to find a better examplification of this creed of fatalism than in the life and activities of one who originated and propounded it—namely, of Mohammed himself. Yet, what do we find in the recorded events of Mohammed's life? A buoyant childhood; an active boyhood; an enterprising period of youth, during which he took part in two commercial ventures necessitating long wearisome journeys of months through the dreary, scorching deserts, a restless manhood given wholly to thinking out the deepest problems of life and destiny, involving an endless travail of the soul, and a protracted middle-age which commenced in comparative calm and ended in perhaps the most strenuous period of his life made up of battles, seiges and expeditions. Such a long and vigorous career

crossed and recrossed by the varied moods and tricks of fortune, does not look like one given to mere passive acceptance of things as they are or to sheer indolent acquiesence in events an they happen, which Fatalism rightly so called, presupposes and enforces. Rather, it has the appearance of a career which believes in actively and courageously working out solely and remaining absolutely resigned to the inscrutable will of God".[4]

Among the factors responsible for the shroud that has rested on the Qur'an, the most striking is the dismal failure on the part of our early doctors of religions who laid the foundations of the medieval Islam which we have inherited to notice what was so clear that the essential purpose of the Qur'an was to explain and interpret to man the *sunnat Allāh* or the ways of Allah; and that for that purpose, it followed a method and a style of its own in the presentation of its subject and employed a diction specifically classified into *muhkamāt* or words be taken in the literal sense and *mutashābihāt* or what were to be conceived figuratively. What absorb the primary attention of these early theologians, however, was not this *sunnah* of Allah but another *sunnah* of the Muslim Arab community, their customs and usages, modelled on what they believed to be the practice of the Prophet, years after the Prophet had passed away—customs and usages of the Arabs codified under several systems of *fiqh*, covering every detail of life. So obsessed were they with this task that they could not give adequate attention to the study and exposition of the *sunnat Allāh* or *fitrat Allāh* or *khalq Allāh* which indeed, according to the Qur'an,, was the 'standard religion'. For, says the Qur'an:

---

[4] Ibid. pp. 50-51.

The Will of God

> *So set thou thy face steadily and truly to the Faith (dīn): (establish) God's handiwork according to the pattern on which He has made mankind (fitrat Allāh): no change (let there be) in the work (wrought) by God (khalq Allāh): that is the standard Religion: but most among mankind understand not.*
>
> *al-Rūm*, 30:30

Note that the terms *fitrat Allāh* and *khalq Allāh* are used precisely in, the same sense, as *sunnat Allāh* or way or course or custom of Allah in 35:43—"No change wilt thou find in God's way (of dealing) (*sunnat Allāh*); no turning off wilt thou find in God's way (of dealing) (*sunnat Allāh*)". This *sunnah*, this course is fixed by Allah to maintain order and harmony in life of not only the entire, universe, but of every object of creation; and the Qur'an takes care to emphasise that this *sunnah* or *khalq Allāh* is indeed *khalq al-Rahmān* or devised not by any "Exalted in Might" or a "Pitiless tyrant" but by "Oft-forgiving" *(al-Mulk,* 67:2) who however transcendent is yet "nearer to him than his jugular vein" (*Qāf*, 50:16) and "listen to the prayer of every suppliant when he calleth on me" (*al-Baqarah*, 2:186). It is this *sunnah* which is the 'Will of God', and man has but to conform to it for a life of peace and order.

As we have pointed out above, the Qur'an follows a method of its own to explain the *Sunnah* of Allah, and employs a diction appropriate to it. *Fadhakkir bil Qur'ān*, "Admonish with the Qur'an" is the directive the Book itself gives (*Qāf*, 50:45). The directive was evidently necessitated by the fact that the Qur'an had primarily to be explained to the unlettered Arabs, of the

Prophet's time among whom and in whose language and idiom it was delivered, and that it had to be explained to them in a manner helpful to a clear grasp of its meaning. States the Qur'an:

> *It is He Who has sent amongst the Unlettered a messenger from among themselves, to rehearse to them His Signs, to sanctify them, and to instruct them in Scripture (kitāb) and wisdom (ḥikmah)—although they had been, before, in manifest error.*
>
> al-Jumuʻah, 62:2

The directive here is to teach or explain the *Kitāb*, the Book or the revelations it contains together with the *Ḥikmah* or the wisdom or purpose underlying them. And this is to be done in a special manner—the manner of the Qur'an. But this manner was never a subject of serious study in any Muslim theological seminar. On the other hand, the early theologians either went by the literal meaning of the word, or were engrossed in applying to the interpretation of the Qur'anic terms, particularly the *mutashābihāt*, the formulae of the scholastic philosophy of Greece after the example of the early Christian theologians, as well as, the dialectic poses which they themselves developed in the name of *ʻilm al-kalām* or dialectic. Indeed, some of them with a mystic bent of mind read strange esoteric meaning into them impelled no doubt by the notion that *ḥikmah* in the phrase *kitāb wal ḥikmah* posited an 'inner meaning' for the words of the Qur'an, and that this was clothed especially in the *mutashābihāt*. That such could not be the normal connotation of the term *ḥikmah* is endorsed by the verse:

> *We sent aforetime Our messengers with clear Signs and sent*

> down with them the Book and the Balance (of Right and Wrong) (kitāb wal mīzān) that men may stand forth in justice.
>
> al-Ḥadīd, 57:25

Here the word *mīzān* or 'Balance' stands in the same relation to the word *kitāb* or 'Book' in the phrase *kitāb wal mīzān* as *ḥikmah* in the phrase *kitāb wal ḥikmah* and must be taken to be synonymous with it in import. *Ḥikmah* is indeed the *mīzān*, the rational basis on which the *kitāb*, the Revelation, is to rest, and help mankind to "stand forth in justice" or live a balanced life. Few paused to consider that the *mutashābihāt* even as the *muḥkamāt* were to be explained primarily to the unlettered folk for whom and among whom and in whose language the revelations were delivered, and that consequently these too were meant to be comprehensible to them in the first instance. A figure of speech, if it has any purpose to serve, has but to reinforce graphically what has been stated in plain words, and hence the *mutashābihāt*, the figurative language, should not have been allowed to mean anything abnormally different from what had been conveyed in the *muḥkamāt* or plain words.

The Qur'an is essentially a moral code of conduct as it expressly claims to be (*al-Baqarah*, 2:2), and as such its method of appeal is necessarily direct. Expressions such as "See things for yourselves and reflect"; "Travel through the earth and see what was the end of those who rejected Truth" (*al-An'ām*, 6:11); "there are indeed Signs for men of understanding" (*Āli 'Imrān*, 3:190); "for those who reflect" (*al-Ra'd*, 13:3); repeating themselves tirelessly at every turn, constitute the manner of that appeal. The method is one of observation, and analogy within the easy grasp of man in every stage of intellectual development. The sense of appreciation may of course vary with every stage of intellect; but the common feature is its easy intelligibility.

The basic concept of life which the Qur'an furnishes is that the entire world of creation and everything contained therein is sustained by certain definite laws inherent in each object and in harmony with each other, that these laws of nature, the *sunnat Allāh*, are necessarily unalterable and that man's joy in life should lie in cooperating with these laws and imitating them in his own activity, assisted by the "proportion and order given to it" (*al-Shams*, 91:7). These laws constitute the 'Will of God' in the phraseology of the Qur'an and man is but to try to the best of his ability to conform to them for a life of peace and order. This, to use the Qur'anic expression is to surrender to His Will (*al-Baqarah*, 2:131).

To bring this fundamental point home, the Qur'an repeatedly draws attention to the indifference of man to see the things which he can clearly see for himself and reflect. The vast panorama of nature, the beautiful constellations moving in the heavens, giving to earth its alternation of day and night, its light and darkness, the soaring clouds that send down rain from the sky to water the earth, the tiny seed that man sows therein shooting out a luxuriant crop affording him his subsistence, the "moist germ" out of which he himself grows into being, and a host of similar familiar objects must, suggest to him that some 'benevolent law' or purpose—*khalq al-Rahmān*—holds together all that he sees or feels through his senses. It emphasises that "not for (idle) sport did We create the heavens and the earth and that is between

The Will of God

them!" (*al-Anbiyā'*, 21:16; *al-Dukhān*, 44:38-39), but for a serious end, that each object of creation is made subject to the laws intrinsic in its nature in order that it might fulfil its function, and that man fitted by nature with a sense of balance and discrimination (*al-Shams*, 91:8) is to conduct himself in accordance with the laws of his own being, and in harmony with the laws governing the rest of creation. "That is the right religion or path of devotion to the ways of Allah," says the Qur'an, and for which "man hath been fitted by his nature", but its regret is that man hath proved 'unjust', 'foolish', and 'hath corrupted the world (*al-Rūm*, 30:41; *al-Aḥzāb*, 33:72).

So, whenever the Qur'an asserts that nothing happens against the Will of God, it only means that the law inherent in the object concerned is at work and has its inevitable course and duration. Man's role on earth is to understand these laws and conform to them; and whenever he neglects to understand and conform to them; the consequence will naturally prove harmful to him. The Qur'anic way of expressing this is: "We have willed it so". In other words: the law must have its course: the cause must produce its effect. That is the scheme of life divinely devised or determined and man is not free to alter that scheme, the 'ways of God'. This is the main domain of life where man has but to conform or surrender to the Will of God or the laws of life which sustain it, if he chooses to profit by them of his own free will.

The Qur'an sometimes speaks of men who refuse to follow the right course and persist in that attitude, and have grown hardened therein. The Book refers to them in this verse: "They have hearts wherewith they understand not, eyes wherewith they see not, and ears wherewith they hear not" (*al-A'rāf*, 7:179). Here again the reference is to the neglect—determined neglect—of the "balance set in the nature of man". The law of life will then have its course, "God hath set a seal on their hearts and on their hearing, and on their eyes is a veil" (*al-Baqarah*, 2:7). That is the Qur'anic style of expressing the consequence.

Sometimes the Qur'an speaks of men who, in their pursuit of a wrong course or in the course of their neglect of some law of life, pause and forsee the nature of the consequence to follow and wish to retrace their steps or resolve to conform to the law which they have so far neglected. Then that law or force so courted acts in them with a revivified vitality to their advantage. Fate or the impending consequence is altered. The process is one of repentance and forgiveness. "He guideth to Himself those who turn to Him in penitence" (*al-Ra'd*, 13:27), or to the laws of life, to God's ways. "If any one earns sin, he earns it against his own soul" (*al-Nisā'*, 4:111), stresses the Qur'an, but adds characteristically: "Your Lord hath inscribed for Himself (the rule of) mercy: verily, if any of you did evil in ignorance, and thereafter repented, and amend (his conduct), lo! He is Oft-forgiving, Most Merciful" (*al-An'ām*, 6:54). "If man but takes one step towards God," adds the Prophet, "God takes two to meet him."[5]

The point to note here is that the initiative for movement and reform should lie with man. That is the law—His Will. So it is with individuals, and so with nations. "Never will God change the condition of a people until they change it themselves

---

5 *Saḥīḥ al-Bukhārī*, "Kitāb al-Tawḥīd", no. 7405, vol. 4, p. 528.

(with their own souls)" (*al-Ra'd*, 13:11).

That such is the meaning or import of the Qur'anic expressions: "We have willed: We have decreed" and so forth with reference to man's freedom to will and act, is unmistakably clear from the following verses which are couched in the plainest language, the *muḥkamāt*, which are to be taken in the literal sense.

Those who strive in Our (Cause)—We will certainly guide them to Our Paths.

al-'Ankabūt, 29:69

Who receiveth guidance, receiveth it for his own benefit: who goeth astray doth so to his own loss: no bearer of burdens can bear the burden of another.

al-Isrā', 17:15

Never will I suffer to be lost the work of any of you, be he male or female.

Āli 'Imrān, 3:195

By the Soul and the proportion and order given to it; And its enlightenment as to its wrong and its right; Truly he succeeds that purifies it, and he fails that corrupts it.

al-Shams, 91:7-10

It must be clear by now, that the Qur'an places no restrictions on man's movement either in thought or knowledge or action save those which should suggest themselves to him through a proper exercise of what the Qur'an calls the 'sense of balance' set in the nature of man. The proviso is of primary importance. One must know one's limits and at the same time appreciate the appropriateness of a move in a given situation. That is the way to exercise the balance properly.

"O Allah! I seek refuge from every desire that cannot be sated and from that prayer that thou may'st not entertain,"[6] is the caution which the Prophet himself observed. This sense of balance or the law of harmony which, as the Qur'an proclaims binds and permeates the entire universe, is in the sphere of human life the supreme moral law which through man's own free will must permeate all his activity both in relation to himself and in relation to his external world, and guide his energies harmoniously to the highest aim. That is the way to "believe and work righteously".

The 'sense of balance' is the unerring force in man to which all his activity is to be referred. It should suggest to him that even as he is to conform to the general laws of nature for a life of order, even so, he is to respect the laws of life that work in his very soul to give inward peace. "On the earth are Signs for those of assured Faith, as also in your own selves" (*al-Dhāriyāt*, 51:20-21). They too constitute the 'will of God' and one is to conform to them also. Conformity implies exertion, and exertion one has to bear if he chooses to move forward from stage to stage (84:19) towards perfection as is the purpose underlying his being. The truth is brought home by a reference to the process of evolution at work in nature.. The seed sown in the earth struggles hard and

---

6 Syed Abdul Latif: *Concept of Society in Islam*, Hyderabad-Deccan, 1937, p. 66.

long against resistance of diverse sorts before it appears in the form of delicious fruit. Even the moist germ which gets into the womb of a prospective mother, what travails does it not pass through before it emerges into its human form! Similarly, observes the Qur'an, man's movement towards moral and spiritual perfection is fraught with inevitable discomfort on the way. The discomfort is to test him and to press him into a better mould. "Be sure We shall test you with something of fear and hunger" (*al-Baqarah*, 2:155); that is the law of existence, His *sunnah*, His habit or practice, and one has to bear it or 'surrender' to it. That is in man's own interest. It will elevate him. To question it is to deny oneself the opportunity of advance.

In the failure to invoke his sense of balance and view life's experience in proper perspective, lie the roots of what man calls 'misery'. This weakness is common to most people; for, deep in the heart of man there dwells a restless thirst for bliss and he expects the world to quench it. Man makes his will the measure of his rights; but the world takes its own course. Disappointment follows, and he "rails at God and Fate."

> "The world's course proves the terms
> On which man wins content;
> Reason the proof confirms—
> We spurn it and invent
> A false course for the world,
> and for ourselves, false powers.

> "Riches we wish to get,
> Yet remain spendthrifts still;
> We would have health, and yet

Still use our bodies ill;
Bafflers of our own prayers, from youth to life's last scenes.

"We would have inward peace,
Yet will not look within;
We would have misery cease,
Yet will not cease form sin;
We want all pleasant ends, but will not use harsh means.

"We do not what we ought,
What we ought not, we do,
And lean upon the thought
That chance will bring us through;
But our own acts, for good or ill,
are mightier powers."—*Enipedocles on Etna*.[7]

The world's course which Enipedocles speaks of here is the law of life, the way of God or His *sunnah*, as the Qur'an styles it. It proves the terms on which man wins content. Reason confirms the proof. But man spurns it and invents for himself a false course. He makes a fool of himself—"A fool of his own woe." Folly brings its own suffering. That is fate, the law of life, the decree God, *taqdīr*. "Whatever misfortune happens to you", points out the Qur'an, it "is because on the things your hands have wrought" (*al-Shūrā*, 42:30).

Fate or *taqdīr* is used in the Qur'an in three broad senses. Firstly, there is the field of what we may term the Divine

---

[7] Matthew Arnold: *Dramatic and Later Poems*, London: Macmillan & Co., 1895, p. 142.

initiative or of the operation of the laws of Nature—*fiṭrat Allāh* or *khalq Allāh* or *sunnat Allāh*. They are signs of a plan of existence necessarily conceived in advance or pre-determined even as every human plan is pre-determined before it is put into action, with this difference that whereas man's knowledge of the nature of things entering his plan being limited, he changes it as experience warrants him, whereas God's knowledge of everything being perfect, occasion cannot arise to alter the course he adopts. God does not alter his ways or the laws of nature or the fundamental bases of life, of its ebbs and flows. They form the exclusive domain of divinity, and man as man has no valid ground to question them, because he cannot grasp in right perspective the working of these laws or the reality about them. He is simply to believe that they are but *khalq al-Raḥmān* or the "laws devised by God, the Lord of Compassion", and must necessarily be good. His responsibility lies only in the nature of the use he makes of these laws. Every reaction to them is *taqdīr*.

Secondly, there is the field of human initiative. "Who receiveth guidance, receiveth it for his own benefit: who goeth astray did so to his own loss" (*al-Isrā'*, 17:15). Our own acts, for good or ill, are mightier powers. That too is *taqdīr*. Man here is the maker of his own fate. The balance set in the nature of man or the sense of discrimination ingrained in him must, in all circumstances, be the final guide in distinguishing between what he ought and what he ought not to do. The Qur'an has laid down certain definite injunctions touching human conduct, as may easily be endorsed by reason and experience. They denote certain principles of life operating for peace and order, and indicate what one has to avoid in life and what to observe. These directions or commandments reflect the principles of harmony subsisting in the world of nature and for that reason may be taken to signify the Will of God, and one has to conform to them also. Conformity with them and non-conformity produce opposite results. Both are styled *taqdīr*.

And lastly, there is the reaction on our life of the deeds of others. Sometimes they bring us joy. The joy may seem unexpected. But the very talent to feel the joy proceeding from the good deeds of others is the result of a process of righteousness in ourselves. Even that is *taqdīr*. Sometimes the deeds of others bring us pain and suffering:

"Though of ours no weakness spoil our lot,
Though the non-human powers of nature harm us not,
The ill-deeds of other men make often our life dark".
—*Empedocles on Etna.*[8]

Taqdīr in this context expresses itself in one of two ways. It may be that those who have thus suffered had not in proper time anticipated the rise of evil tendencies in others, and exercised proper check on them, by every reasonable means open to them or to use the Qur'anic phrase "did not restrain wrong doing", or it may be that they knowingly abstained from interference. They have to pay the penalty for the failure to do so. This holds good in domestic as well as national and international life. Much of the suffering in this world, including the suffering wrought by wars is preventable by people who through indifference or a false sense of tolerance which in certain

---

8 Matthew Arnold: *op. cit.*, p. 144.

situations amounts to criminal unconcern with what is going on around them, allow evil to prosper. Suffering is the result not merely for the wrong doer but also for those seemingly innocent, who have failed to prevent wrong doing, That is the law of life or *taqdīr*. Neglect of duty to check evil in time in others is in reality participation in the evil.

Here comes in the injunction of the Qur'an, the injunction designated as *jihād*, another term which, as *kufr* already noticed, has come to be an odium among non-Muslim circles not fully conversant with the Qur'anic connotation of it. The term literally means 'exertion' or striving against all that is evil, whether in thought, or feeling or action. That is an essential condition of a peaceful life; so much so, that the highest and the most trying form of it is the *jihād* against one's own evil ways. To fight evil desire rising from within and let life run on lines which bring inward peace is by no means an easy affair. Fighting with arms those who are out to disturb the peace of the world or bent on the destruction of the good in life is *jihād*, as commonly understood, but the *jihād* with one's own self is indeed a hard task. Hence it is called '*al-jihād al-akbar*', the greatest of *jihāds*. To abstain from this *jihād* in one's own personal case is to let the 'self' disintegrate. Likewise to abstain from remonstrating with the evil around by thought or deed as the case may demand or warrant, is to be a party to the disintegration of corporate happiness for man. The ill-deeds of other men involve us in the result of their ill-deeds whenever we abstain from putting a check on them. The question of one's life getting dark on that account shall not arise as Empedocles fancies it does. It is on the other hand a penalty one has to pay for letting others freely to indulge in evil deeds.

There is another side to this very problem. We remonstrate against evil. We exert and do *jihād* against it. The utmost what one should do is done, and yet evil triumphs bringing suffering with it. Even that is *taqdīr*. But that should not 'darken our life' as such a feeling would betray the sense of frustration and defeatism in life. The Qur'an warns us against the growth of that feeling. One is to bear it and turn failure to moral victory. That is righteous action or *'amal sālih*.

By Time, verily, Man is in loss, except such as have Faith, and do righteous deeds, and (join together) in the mutual teaching of Truth, and of Patience and Constancy.

al-'Asr, 103:1-3

Be sure We shall test you with something of fear and hunger, some loss in goods or lives or the fruits (of your toil).

al-Baqarah, 2:155

The suffering involved in the upholding of truth is a test and these who bear the ordeal elevate themselves in the scale of life and enter the ranks of the *sābirīn* or those who endure. The ordeal is implicit in the march onward from state to state towards Reality.

It was in a situation like this, that Christ in the agony of his soul on the night at Gethsmane cried out, "O my Father! If it be possible, let this cup pass from me. Nevertheless, not as I will, but as thou Wilt"[9]—words worthy of a Prince among the *Ṣābirīn*; those who endure steadfastly.

Lastly, when all is said on the subject that what is called *taqdīr* is in some form or other the name for a stage in the process of human activity, the Qur'an reserves to God a realm of activity on which man as man has no meaning to enter—the realm of 'Divine Veto'. However, endowed with knowledge, however circumspect, man cannot always be certain of the result he anticipates. A stage does come when all that is humanly possible is done, and yet the result is not as anticipated or to one's liking. In the world of morals and of moral justice, the good intention is what matters and must bring its own satisfaction. That is one's real reward. In the material sphere the result may not be pleasing at first; but God knows what its final form is to be.

It is possible that ye dislike a thing which is good for you, and that ye love a thing which is bad for you. But God knoweth, and ye know not.

al-Baqarah, 2:216

To God do belong the unseen (secrets) of the heavens and the earth, and to Him goeth back every affair (for decision). The worship Him and put thy trust in Him: and thy Lord is not unmindful of aught that ye do.

Hūd, 11:123

The task then before man is to do a thing that be right and

---

9 *The New Testament*: St. Matthew, 26:39.

leave the rest to God. He has but to conform his way to the ways of God, his will to the divine will and to bear and endure the ordeals of life with truth and steadfastness. That is the cardinal message of the Qur'an.

After all, life on this side of the grave is not the whole of it. The life beyond also matters. It is a continuation of it. "Your creation and your resurrection is in no wise but as an individual soul" (*Luqmān*, 31:28). The result of one's good deeds may not be discernible in this life; but it will be crystal clear in the next. Only, man has to do all that is possible for him to do to live in conformity with the will and ways of God leaving the rest to Him, in fervent love and trust and hope. That is the way to live in Islam. No wonder Goethe exclaimed. "If this be *Islam*, do we not all live in *Islam*,"[10] and Carlyle, a soul akin to Goethe echoed the cry:

"I say, this is yet the only true morality known. A man is right and invincible, virtuous and on the road towards sure conquest, precisely while he joins himself to the great Law of the World, in spite of all superficial laws, temporary appearances, profit-and-loss calculations; he is victorious while he cooperates with that great Law, not victorious otherwise;—and surely his first chance of cooperating with it, or getting into the course of it, is to know with his whole soul that it is;, that it is good, and alone good! This is the soul of Islam; and it is probably the soul of Christianity".[11]

---

10 Quoted by Carlyle in *On Heroes, Hero Worship, and the Heroic in History*, new edition prepared by Micheal K Goldberg *et. al.*, University of California Press, 1993, p. 49.

11 Ibid.

Asks the Qur'an:
When whither go ye?
Verily this is no less than a Message to (all) the Worlds
(With profit) to whoever among you wills to go straight
But ye shall not will except as God wills—
the Cherisher of Worlds.
al-Takwīr, 81:26-29

How then is one to will as God willeth, or to join to the great Law of the World?

CHAPTER 5
Al-'Amal al-Ṣāliḥ

IT MUST be clear by now that human life, according to the Qur'an, is to express itself in a system of activity promoting peace and harmony in life, and that subject to that end in view and in conformity with the principles underlying it, man has every freedom to will and act. And there is the assurance to every individual:

> On no soul doth God place a burden greater than it can bear.
>
> al-Baqarah, 2:286

According to the Qur'an, man has a dual responsibility to discharge. One is in relation to himself, the other is in relation to his external world. The one is to acknowledge in thought and action what is styled as *ḥuqūq Allāh* or the rights of God; the other is to acknowledge equally well *ḥuqūq al-'ibād* or *ḥuqūq an-nās*, or the rights of the external world of creation. The former has to express itself in a process of self-development—physical, intellectual and spiritual. In other words, man's primary responsibility is to invite God, so to say, exercise His right to dwell in the individual and urge him to use properly the balance set in his nature. The idea is in conformity with the

Al-'Amal al-Sāliḥ

Qur'anic exhortation:
O ye who believe! If ye will aid (the cause of) God, He will aid you, and plant your feet firmly.
Muḥammad, 47:7

The other responsibility lies in developing social conscience and in caring for the welfare of others. This is respecting in one's life and activity the rights of others. The two terms may as well be styled as 'obligations to one's self' and 'obligations to society'. The two types of responsibilities are not to be regarded as exclusive. They are merely two facets of one and the same attitude towards life, of the same activity proceeding from it and signify the character of the mind one has to develop. It is this mind which matters in determining responsibility for every human action. "Actions rest on motives",[1] says the Prophet, because motive is the index to the mind or to the manner in which the mind chooses to exercise the balance set in the nature of man and expresses itself in action. It is why every stress is laid on purity of motives. And this purity is promoted by a proper exercise of the 'balance' aiming at a harmonious blending of the *ḥuqūq Allāh* with the *ḥuqūq al-'ibād* or the obligations to self with the obligations to society, or by identifying one's own interests with the interests of the world at large. Such is *'amal al-ṣāliḥ* or righteous work.

The culture of Islam is but an expression of this process. The directive inspiring the process is summed up in the words of the Prophet: "Respect the ways of God and be affectionate to the

---

[1] *Saḥīḥ al-Bukhārī*, "Kitāb Bad' al-Wahi", *ḥadīth* no. 1, vol. 1, p. 3.

family of God".[2] The obligations to one's self and the obligations to others are here placed side by side to form integral aspects of one's activity in life. Whatever one's role either in one's family circle, or in society at large, one has to be mindful of this dual responsibility. To be so mindful is *khayr* or 'Good' and not to be so mindful is *sharr* or 'Evil'. The distinction is to be upheld in every sphere of life's activity—physical, intellectual, spiritual, social, economic and political. It is this distinction which underlies also the principle distinguishing the *ḥalāl*, the permissible or the lawful from the *ḥarām* or unlawful, and which also forms the basis of the injunction calling upon man to "enjoin the right conduct and forbid the wrong". The distinction applies to individual, as well as to corporate life, and cuts across both *ḥuqūq Allāh* and *ḥuqūq al-'ibād*. Righteous work in the context of the commandment "Believe and work righteously" has no other meaning for man except to bear this distinction in mind in all activity, whether it concerns his own self or his relations with his fellow beings or his conduct towards dumb creatures. The personal virtues of kindliness, purity, chastity, love, affection, truth, respect for covenants, forbearance, forgiveness, trustworthiness, justice, mercy and the like are not mere luxuries to be indulged in at convenience but are indispensable for a righteous living. And the opposite qualities such as hate, cruelty, indecency, fornication, adultery, dishonesty, falsehood, treachery, hypocrisy, spite, defection, unfaithfulness, and exploitation of the weak which work for the disintegration of society are not only vices but positive sins in Islam, and are therefore not merely to

---

2 See note 1, p. vii.

be strenuously avoided but firmly discountenanced.

Such is the wide interpretation given by the Qur'an to *'amal al-sāliḥ* or righteous work—work that helps man to live in peace with himself and in peace with his fellow beings and the rest of creation. To so live is to live in Islam which itself means 'Peace'—peace realized in the devotion of all our faculties to the Will of God which as we have explained already, is nothing but the law of life devised in His infinite goodness to work for harmony expressive of the unity of existence. The duty of every Muslim is to see that every little act of his conforms to this law of harmonious living.

Truly, my prayer and service of sacrifice, my life and my death, are (all) for God.

al-An'ām, 6:162

Life thus viewed, every action of man assumes a spiritual significance. It is this significance which distinguishes *'amal al-sāliḥ* from every other form of human activity. The spirit underlying it, whatever the field of expression, the *ḥuqūq Allāh* or *ḥuqūq al-'ibād*, is the result of a harmonious interaction of the twin spiritual faculties in man—the sense of God, and the sense of fellow-feeling. It is this which supplies the emotional background to the display in every situation of a third faculty, the sense of "balance set in his nature"—essentially an intellectual force—and gives to the resultant action the quality of righteousness which the Qur'an speaks of. To pursue the path of righteousness or of *'amal al-sāliḥ* is in reality to respect the ways of Allah, and to show affection to the 'family of Allah' or in the phrase of Carlyle to join to the "Great law of the world". It is along this path that we meet the *ṣāliḥīn* and the *muttaqīn*, the *ṣābirīn*, the *ūlu'l-abṣār* and the *ūlu'l-albāb* and the rest of the noble types, of men and women who form the very salt of the earth. Whenever the devout Muslim raises his voice in his prayer to God to say "show us the right path, the path of those whom Thou hast blessed", it is this path of true righteousness or *'amal al-ṣāliḥ* that he desires to be shown and guided therein. The highest aim which a nation or community may, on the analogy of the individual, aspire to is not material or political superiority over others as seems to have had a fascination for ambitious people throughout history. The very idea of a distinction on this basis between one community and another is excluded from the concept of international life favoured by Islam, the concept of a "fold, every member of which shall be a shepherd or keeper unto every other". The criterion of superiority must lie in the character of the corporate righteousness displayed. Prayed the Prophet both for himself and his followers:

> "O Allah! Make us guides in the path of Life, and keep us guided ourselves therein—neither going astray, nor leading astray".[3]

An attitude such as this is possible when one has blended his sense of *ḥuqūq Allāh* with that of *ḥuqūq an-nās* or *ḥuqūq al-'ibād*, an attitude in the development of which everyone is recommended by the Prophet to seek divine help:

> "O Allah! I seek Thy refuge from misleading others, and from being misled by others; from betraying others into error, and from being betrayed into error by others; from doing any wrong to

---

3 Syed Abdul Latif: *Concept of Society in Islam, op. cit.*, pp. 73-74.

others; and from being wronged by others; and from drawing others into ignorance, and from being drown into ignorance by others.[4]

"O Allah! I seek Thy refuge from any wrong that I may do to others, and from any wrong that others may do to me, from any harshness that I may show to others, and from any harshness that others may show to me; and from any sin that Thou mayst not forgive".[5]

I have quoted from the prayers of the Prophet just to reach by the quickest route the mind favoured of the Qur'an; for, a prayer is the surest index to the mind of one who prays. It affords an insight into the working of his mind, his thoughts and feelings and the very object of his life. There is no prevarication, no hiding or suppression of truth, no luxurious display of poetic fancy when man stands face to face with the Creator of his being to lay bare before Him his heart, and give an account of his mundane struggles, his achievements and disappointments, and to ask of him the things that matter. His prayer, at such a moment, is an expression of a pressing feeling, and is for that reason naturally simple and direct. The note that he strikes in his outpourings points to the character of the mind that he has developed.

In Islam, the prayer that one offers whether singly or in congregation, whether at the appointed hours of devotion or at any sudden call or urge from within to turn to his Lord in the

---

4 Ibid. p. 72.

5 Ibid. p. 73.

midst of his daily work is all couched in the phraseology of the Qur'an or that of the Prophet's own utterances preserved in the *hadīth*. Even when the supplicant expresses himself in his own tongue, the form of prayer is dictated by the same source. The same attitude toward his Master, the same conception behind the words used, the same spiritual atmosphere generated by them are revived in his mind, and nothing that he says is not covered by the teachings of the Qur'an and the example of the Prophet.

"O Allah! Make Islam most pleasing to me",[6] is one of the Prophet's prayers. It is a brief utterance; yet, how comprehensive! The supplicant here asks for the path of Islam to be smoothed for him, to be made most pleasing—the path of Islam which is the path of devotion, of strenuous struggle with evil and of bringing our own will into accord with the Supreme Will, or of devoting all our talents to the service of the highest in life. He asks for a life disciplined in the ways of Allah or the laws intrinsic in our nature working for peace. It is a duty in the discharge of which few there are who can claim not to have faltered. Yet, a true Muslim is to ask of God to make such a trying task most pleasing to him.

It is towards this end that every prayer of Islam is directed. Mark the character of the following two prayers which have found their way into the regular daily worship of a Muslim. One is the common prayer of Islam and the most compulsory with which every service begins, and the other is what enters into his vespers:

Praise be to God, the Cherisher and Sustainer of the

---

6 Ibid. p. 65.

Worlds; Most Gracious, Most Merciful; Master of the Day of Judgement; Thee do we worship, and Thine aid we seek. Show us the straight way; the way of those on whom Thou hast bestowed Thy Grace, those whose (portion) is not wrath, and who go not astray.
al-Fātiḥah, 1:1-7

This prayer repeated several times every day serves as a recurrent reminder to a Muslim of the character of life that he is to pursue—a life of righteous conduct. The same note is struck in his vespers:

> "O Allah! Guide me to be of those whom Thou hast guided and preserve me to be of those whom Thou hast preserved, and befriend me to be of those whom Thou hast befriended, and bless me in what Thou doth grant me, and protect me from the evil of everything that Thou mayst prescribe for me; for surely, Thou alone canst prescribe what Thou desireth, and none can over-rule Thee. Surely, he whom Thou befriendeth is never disgraced. Blessed art Thou, our Lord, and Exalted!"[7]

It must be noted that every Islamic prayer is a resolve to conform with Divine aid to the ways of God or *sunnat Allāh* in order that one might dischrage one's obligations to one's own self and one's obligations to others—the *ḥuqūq Allāh* and the *ḥuqūq al-'ibād*.

> "I ask of thee the qualities which move Thy grace and forgiveness. I ask of thee protection from doing harm to any one and I ask of

---

7 *Concept of Society in Islam*, op. cit., p. 63.

thee the chance of doing good to everyone".[8]

"O Allah! I ask of thee steadfastness in every pursuit. I ask of Thee the intent for good action and the power to thank Thee for Thy benevolence and to render Thee devoted service. I ask of Thee the tongue that speaketh truth, and the mind that erreth not and the gift of true fellow-feeling. I seek Thy refuge from the evil of everything that Thou knoweth; and I ask of Thee the good that lieth in everything that Thou knoweth; and I seek Thy refuge from every sin of which Thou hast knowledge. And verily Thou knoweth all that we cannot know".[9]

Note the spirit of the following prayer:

"O Allah! Improve my spiritual life, for that is to be my refuge; and purify my material life for I have to live it, and prepare me for the life to which I shall have to return; and keep me alive till it is good for me to be alive, and call me back when it is good for me to die. Lengthen my life in every goodly state, and turn death into bliss before any evil state supervenes".[10]

Death should thus have no terror for man. What one should fear is wickedness or evil life; and it is against this that one has to seek Divine protection. In whatever man may ask for, he is never to forget his primary need for purity of life.

"O Allah! Bless me always with the joy of Thy sight and the pleasure of beholding Thy countenance unharmed by anything

---

8 Ibid. p. 69.

9 Ibid. pp. 70-71.

10 Ibid. pp. 63-64.

Al-'Amal al-Ṣāliḥ

harmful and undisturbed by anything disturbing.[11]

"O Allah! I ask of Thee a pure life, and a pure death, and a returning unto Thee that shall not call for reprehension or disgrace".[12]

The prayers given above, as all others contained in the Qur'an and the *ḥadīth*, reveal the yearning of a type of mind every move of which is directed by an all absorbing sense of God on the one hand, and by an equally powerful sense of responsibility resting on it on the other, to render in a life hereafter an account of its activity in the present.

The thought of this life hereafter which according to the Qur'an is "life indeed" (*al-'Ankabūt*, 29:64) is to be kept so constantly in view that the present is to be regarded as but a preparation for it, and for that reason raised, as already observed, to the position of a cardinal belief in Islam as important to the life of man as every other cardinal belief to be expressed in righteous work or *'amal al-ṣāliḥ*.

---

11 Ibid. p. 73.

12 Ibid. p. 64.

CHAPTER 6
Life Hereafter

IN SOME form or other, the belief in the life hereafter is common to all Faiths. What that Life in reality is can be known only when one enters upon it. It is certainly not a return to earth again or what is called a 'rebirth' in flesh and blood. Life according to the Qur'an is not a cycle. It is a linear line and is to "express itself every moment in fresh glory" (*al-Raḥmān*, 55:29). The description of the 'life to follow' given in the stories which have found their way into the *ḥadīth* literature and which have exercised a fascination for the medieval mind among Muslims has, except in a few cases, no parallel in the Qur'an. The Qur'anic method is to convey just a vision of it, and that by means of what are specifically called *amthāl* and *mutashābihāt*, parables, similitudes and metaphors, essentially symbolic in import; for, the life beyond is something which man in his present environment can scarcely comprehend or understand.

The vision conveyed by means of *amthāl* and *mutashābihāt* is intended to be satisfying to the intellect alike of men of insight and of the less gifted. The righteous shall have a life of peace and the unrighteous of disquiet. That is the impression which they are meant to convey. And as the similitudes offered are necessarily to be drawn from the life of comfort known, the picture of comfort provided is that of gardens beneath which rivers flow, of fountains of milk and honey, of pleasant society and so forth. But there is always a corrective to the picture clinching the vision. The gardens of Heaven are different from those of this world. The fruits are not subject to seasons (*al-Ra'd*, 13:35). The water of rivers does not petrify: it tastes differently (*Muhammad*, 47:15). The companions are not set in corporal frame, they are made of purity, and do not age (*al-Baqarah*, 2:25). They do not hold vain discourse (*Maryam*, 19:62). The entire vision is rounded up by a *hadīth al-qudsī*, which emphasises that these *amthāl* or similitudes cannot afford even a glimpse of reality: "God says: He has prepared for his righteous servants what no eye hath seen and no ear hath heard and no mind of man hath conceived".[1]

Likewise the *amthāl* touching the life in Hell all drawn from the field of corporeal suffering are meant to symbolize the condition in which the soul of the unrighteous will find itself in its new setting. The Qur'an itself affords clarification. "What will convey to thee what the Consuming Fire (Hell) is?" asks the Qur'an; and itself furnishes the answer: "It is the Fire of (the Wrath of) God kindled (to a blaze), which doth mount (right) to the Hearts" (*al-Humazah*, 104:5-7). The verse likens Hell to a mind in spiritual distress.

The picture of Heaven and Hell, which the Qur'an conveys through its *amthāl* is that of two different states of the human

---

[1] *Sahīh al-Bukhārī*, "Kitāb Bad' al-Khalq", *hadīth* no. 3244, vol. 2, part 4, p. 424; *Sahīh Muslim*, "Kitāb al-Jannah wa Sifātihā", *hadīth* no. 2824, vol. 4, p. 2174.

soul set in an environment different from that in which its present life is lived. A conversation of the Prophet with a messenger from Heracleus, recorded by Imām Fakhruddīn Rāzī in his *al-Tafsīr al-Kabīr* under verse 3:127 throws light on the view advanced. Referring to the verse "Be quick in the race for forgiveness from your Lord and for a Garden whose width is that (of the whole) of the heavens and of the earth prepared for the righteous" (*Āli 'Imrān*, 3:133), the Roman representative asked: "Where does Hell exist if Paradise extends over the heavens and the earth?" Quietly the Prophet parried: "Glory be to Allah: Where is the night when the day comes?"[2]

I may proceed a step further. According to the Qur'an every one will have to pass through Hell (*Maryam*, 19:71). It is contended by the orthodox commentators that the text refers to a bridge over Hell which, as stated in a *hadīth*,[3] one has to cross on the Day of Judgement—an idea which curiously runs parallel to what prevailed in early Zoroastrianism.[4] The Qur'an, may it be pointed out, makes no mention of such a bridge whatsoever. Even so, the contention that Hell and Heaven are but two dinerent states of the soul in the life hereafter is upheld by the very

---

2 Fakhruddīn al-Rāzī: *al-Tafsīr al-Kabīr*, Istanbul: al-Matba'ah al-Amīriyyah, 1308 AH., vol. 3, p. 75.

3 *Sahīh al-Bukhārī*, "Kitāb al-Adhān", no. 764; "Kitāb al-Tawhīd", no. 6885; *Sahīh Muslim*, "Kitāb al-Īmān", nos. 267 and 286; *Sunan Abū Dāwūd*, "Kitāb al-Sunnah", no. 4128.

4 Duncan Greenlees: *The Gospel of Zarathushtra*, Adyar: The Theosophical Publishing House, 1951, pp. 124-138.

ḥadīth which provides a bridge across Hell: for, to the Faithful, Hell will say: "Cross the bridge, O true believer, for thy light hath put out my fire". The issue is clarified by Jalāluddin Rūmī, the poet and mystic in his *Mathnawī* II, 2554-2568:

"At the gathering for judgement the Faithful will say,
'O Angel, is not Hell the common road,
Trodden by the believer and the infidel alike?
Yet we saw not any smoke or fire on our way'.
Then the Angel will reply: 'That garden which ye saw
as ye passed,
Was indeed Hell, but unto you it appeared a pleasance of
greenery.
'Since ye strove against the flesh and quenched the flames of lust
for God's sake,
So that they became verdant with holiness and lit the path to
salvation:
Since ye turned the fire of wrath to meekness, and Murky
ignorance to radiant knowledge;
Since ye made the fiery soul (*nafs*) an orchard where nightingales
of prayer and praise were ever singing,
So, hath Hell-fire become for you greenery and roses and riches
without end'".[5]

Whatever the nature of Hell or Heaven, it is to be admitted that life in either sphere must eventually subserve an ultimate divine purpose common to all mankind who according to the Qur'an mark a distinct stage in creative evolution. For, it is clear that Hell and Heaven whether they are mere states of the soul or

---

5 Rūmī, *Selections*, by R.A. Nicholson, London: George Allen and Unwin Ltd., 1930.

otherwise cannot remain so for all times. That would be stagnation and the stultifying of the purpose of evolution. Hence it is that the Qur'an takes care to disclose the purpose. "Ye shall surely travel from stage to stage" (*al-Inshiqāq*, 84:19). It is a promise held out to the righteous and the unrighteous alike. And how is this to be fulfilled?

The Qur'an makes it repeatedly clear that the righteous on earth and the unrighteous will have to carry with him to the next stage in life the reactions of his deeds indelibly impressed on his soul. His action, his thought, his speech, his feeling, his imagination—nay, even his fancy will cling to his neck tenaciously and mark the character of the life he has lived.

> *Every man's fate We have fastened on his own neck: on the Day of Judgement We shall bring out for him a scroll, which he will see spread open. (It will be said to him:) "Read thine (own) record: sufficient is thy soul this day to make out an account against thee."*
>
> *al-Isrā'*, 17:13-14

In ways peculiar to the new stage of life will every one be made to realise the beauty or the ugliness of the life he has pursued in the past, but which through ignorance, perversity or willful disregard of the 'Signs of God', he had refused to see for himself while he had still the time and opportunity to make amends guided by the "balance set in his nature". The beauty of his past life or its ugliness is brought face to face with him in the stage after death in a form which in his fresh set-up he will behold with joy or look upon in helpless anguish.

In the Qur'anic view, the life beautiful is to march onward

towards perfection. Likewise, the life ugly has first its own process of purification to go through. For the one, there is freedom of movement, for the other, there is the handicap of the self to overcome. The situation of the one is styled as *qurb*, nearness to God: the other, *bu'd* or distance from God. It is this distance which is but a reflection of its unrighteous life on earth, the distance so to say that he had assumed towards God in his earthly life. "Those who were blind in this world, will be blind in the Hereafter, and most astray from the Path" (*al-Isrā'*, 17:72). It is the resultant distance from the very 'countenance of God' that will be galling to the soul of man. To use the scriptural terms it would be 'Hell' for him as 'Heaven' for the other. "The most favoured of men", said the Prophet, "will be he who shall see his Lord's countenance and His Glory, night and day, a felicity which shall surpass all the pleasures of the body as the ocean surpasses a drop of perspiration".

In this connection let me observe that in the Qur'anic sense Hell and Heaven begin for man in this life; for whatever good he does or evil, at once becomes part of him and begins to give him a foretaste of Heaven or Hell to follow. The good dead will promote spiritual elevation; the evil deed, its own downward feeling. If man could not realise the ugliness of his deed before his death and feel sincerely repentant, and retrace his steps, there is always the grace of God to bring him peace of mind.

And indeed We will make them taste of the Penalty of this (life) prior to the supreme Penalty, in order that they may (repent and) return.

al-Sajdah, 32:21

He is the One That accepts repentance from His servants and forgives sins: and He knows all that ye do.
                                                    al-Shūrā, 42:25

That is the way to burn out impurities or pass through Hell in order to fit oneself to enter Heaven. Realisation of the ugliness of sin is naturally painful. It is mortal acid spiritual torture, or, in the language of the Qur'an 'Hellfire'. The process of purification is needed not merely for the habitual transgressors but even for those essentially righteous who at times fall off the righteous track; for, no human being is infallible. In their case, while they are equipped in every other way to enjoy freedom of movement towards perfection, they will have to drop before their march begins that which would retard their progress. In the imagery of the Qur'an, they have to enter heaven by a passage through Hell, even as others (*Maryam*, 19:71). The essentially righteous finish this course in their present life by a painful realisation of the nature of whatever error they might have fallen into. It is a process of repentance in time and of forgiveness and of spiritual cleansing before death. It is to them will the words be addressed:

O (thou) soul, in (complete) rest and satisfaction!
Come back thou to thy Lord—well-pleased (thyself) and well-pleasing unto Him!
Enter thou, then, among My devotees!
Yea, enter thou My Heaven
                                                    al-Fajr, 89:27-30

They will have no further need to pass through this mill of purification, for they have already gone through it in their present life. The process will certainly await those who have deliberately neglected their opportunities while they had the time to do so. It is they who shall have to pass in their next stage through the ordeal and in the language of a *ḥadīth*, 'made clean' before they are allowed to enter Heaven to resume their march towards perfection.

"Ye shall surely travel from stage to stage", is then the plan of life, as visualised by the Qur'an. The 'life beautiful', will be carried forward from stage to stage till it reaches perfection or 'beholds the very vision of God'. The 'life ugly' naturally will lag behind, and have to make up a long leeway before it can emerge into the life of free movement. How long the process of purification will last is a matter with God. The term *abad*, loosely rendered into English as 'Eternal' on the analogy of the Judaic and Christian concept is in the Qur'anic sense just a period appropriate to the sin requiring purgation as fixed by God according to His own sense of time and His own sense of values. Else we shall have to face the Thought of 'duality', or a multiplicity of undying units possessing or claiming the quality of coexistence in eternity with God, a thought running counter to the Qur'anic concept of *Tawḥīd*, as also to the assertion of the Qur'an that all created objects shall have an end one day. Surely, Hell and Heaven and man enter the list.

That such is the meanings implied by the term *abad* is used by the Qur'an in respect of the process of purification in Hell is manifest from the more explicit terms used to specify the duration. Verses 22 and 23 of chapter 78 speak of Hell as a "home of transgressors to abide therein *for years*". *Aḥqāb* is the term here used which is plural of *ḥuqūb* which according to the *Arabic-English Lexicon* by E.W. Lane means a period which may range from one year to eighty years, denoting at best a long time. Again, verses 109-110 of chapter 11 of the Qur'an discountenance the idea of a life in Hell without end. Here, while the blessed shall abide in Paradise "as long as the Heavens and the earth endure which whatever imperishable boon thy Lord may please to add", life in Hell "shall last as long as the Heavens and the Earth endure unless thy Lord willeth otherwise; Verily thy Lord doeth what He chooseth". Note that life in Hell and Paradise cannot be eternal, since it cannot survive the Heavens and the Earth which have one day to disappear. Note also the phrase "unless thy Lord willeth otherwise", and view it in the light of the interpretation given to the 'Will of God' in chapter 4 of this volume, and it will be clear that life in Hell is to be commensurate one's transgressions in this life. For, indeed, this such is the import of the phrase, is clear from the following verses:

> *He that doeth good shall have ten times as much to his credit: he that doeth evil shall only be recompensed according to his evil: no wrong shall be done unto (any of) them.*
>
> *al-An'ām*, 6:160

Every ordeal in Hell to be undergone in consequence of an evil action has thus a limit set to it. For, to prolong the agony beyond the limit warranted by the character of evil done or for ever will clearly be injustice, and the verse promises that "none

shall be treated unjustly the Qur'an". Adds the Qur'an:
> God is never unjust in the least degree: if there is any good (done), He doubleth it, and giveth from His own presence a great reward.
>
> al-Nisā', 4:40

The general attitude towards the problem of Hell, not withstanding the graphic symbolism employed to reveal the hideousness of sin and its consequences, is one of pity transformed into an ultimate force for mercy. "My mercy triumphs over my displeasure", says God, according to a *ḥadīth al-qudsī* of the Prophet.[6] The Qur'an itself records the divine affirmation: "My mercy encompasseth everything." And that should help one to reject once for all the theory of an eternal Hell so strongly upheld even today by our orthodox theologians. Let me quote a few *ḥadīths* of the Prophet in support of the contention.

Imām Muslim records a *ḥadīth* touching those for whom none will come forward to intercede on the Day of Judgement and for whom through His own infinite sense of mercy will God declare Himself the intercessor:

> "Allah will then say: The angels and the Prophet and the faithful, they will have interceded for the sinners and now there remains none to intercede for them except the most merciful of all merciful ones. So, He will take out a handful from fire and bring out a people who never worked any good".[7]

---

6 *Ṣaḥīḥ al-Bukhārī*, "Kitāb Bad' al-Khalq", *ḥadīth* no. 3194 (vol. 4, p. 409), and "Kitāb at-Tawḥīd".

7 *Ṣaḥīḥ Muslim*, "Kitāb al-Īmān", *ḥadīth* No. 269.

Kanz al-Ummal records two sayings of the Prophet:
"Surely a day will come over Hell, when it will be like a field of corn that has dried up after flourishing for a while.
"Surely a day will come over Hell when there shall not be a single human being in it".[8]

In the *Sihāh* there are on record the following sayings of the Prophet:
1. "When a period will pass over the inmates of Hell, the Lord Compassionate will put his foot on it and Hell will break down and disappear".[9]
2. "Hell will always desire more and more sinners to pour in but a time will come when God the Almighty will thrust his foot into it to see if that could not satisfy it. When Lo! Hell will cry out 'Enough, enough! I seek refuge in Thy Might and in Thy compassion' and will cease to exist. Heaven will always have a vast unoccupied space. God will people it by a new type of people who will thereafter dwell therein".[10]

The idea is to let the inmates of Hell pass on into Heaven after they have gone, through a process of purification.

That the companions of the Prophet were aware of this attitude of the Prophet towards the problem of Hell, may be

---

8 *Kanz al-Ummal*, Hyderabad-Deccan: Dā'irat-ul-Ma'ārif, vol. III, p. 245, No. 279-291.

9 *Sahīh Muslim*, "Kitāb al-Jannah wa Sifāti Na'īmihā wa Ahluhā", *hadīths* No. 5084-5085.

10 *Sahīh al-Bukhārī*, "Kitāb at-Tawhīd".

gathered from a saying of Caliph 'Umar recorded in *Fath al-Bayān*, *Fath al-Bārī*, *al-Durr al-Manthūr* and *Hādī al-Arwāh* of Ibn al-Qayyūm which runs:

"Even though the dwellers in Hell may be numberless as the sands of the desert, a day will surely come when they will be taken out of it".[11]

The notes of warning in the Qur'an against sinful life and the description of the consequences to follow which, form part of the *kitāb* have a *hikmah* attached to them. This *hikmah* or purpose is obviously to create in man the sense of horror for sin. They are there to desist him from it, and to induce in him the sence of repentance if he is already involved therein. Repentance is sure to meet with forgiveness; for, God is oft-forgiving, oft-returning and gracious is He to those who return to him. The idea is to eliminate from human life every form of resistance which sin offers to spiritual development or purity of life. To realise the nature of sin and to resolve to make amends is no doubt a trying process. But it is better one goes through it here rather than in the hereafter, where in the stage of transition called *barzakh*, one will have to realise the hideousness of sin and burn out all impurities attached to one's soul on its account. This process of purification is an expression of Divine mercy. The sooner the man repents whether here or there, the earlier is the dawn of forgiveness on him in either setting. The everlasting consignment to Hell is repugnant to the *hikmah* underlying all references to sin

---

11 *The Holy Qur'an with Commentary* by Moulvi Mohammad Ali, p. 472.

and its consequences. That will be arguing against the principle of movement implicit in the verse "Ye shall surely travel from stage to stage". At the same time it will be imposing a limit on the exercise of Divine mercy. God definitely refuses to agree to any limit:

> *O my servants who have transgressed against their souls! Despair not of the mercy of God: for God forgiveth all sins: for He is Oft-forgiving, Most Merciful.*
>
> al-Zumar, 39:53

The principle of movement "from stage to stage" is brought to mind repeatedly by the Qur'an to warn who would not believe in death opening a new life. The Book reminds man of the most obscure conditions in which his first life began and emphasises that as even from a lower stage to a higher, man's development has been marked, even so, after death the movement upward will continue.

> *It is He That created you in diverse stages*
>
> Nūḥ, 71:14

> *And God has produced you*
> *from the earth growing (gradually);*
> *And in the end He will return you into the (earth)*
> *And raise you forth (again at the Resurrection).*
>
> Nūḥ, 71:17-18

> *From the (earth) did We create you, and into it shall We return you, and from it shall We bring you out once again.*
>
> Ṭā Hā, 20:55

Man We did create from a quintessence (of clay);
Then We placed him as (a drop of) sperm
in a place of rest, firmly fixed;
Then We made the sperm into a clot of congealed blood;
Then of that clot We made a (foetus) lump;
Then We made out of that lump bones
and clothed the bones with flesh;
Then We developed out of it another creature.
So blessed be God, the Best to create!
After that, at length ye will die,
Again on the Day of Judgement, will ye be raised up.
al-Mu'minūn, 23:12-16

He Who has made everything
which He has created most good:
He began the creation of man
with (nothing more than) clay,
And made his progeny from a quintessence
of the nature of a fluid despised:
But He fashioned him in due proportion,
and breathed into him something of His spirit.
And He gave you (the faculties of) hearing and sight
and feeling (and understanding): little thanks do ye give!
al-Sajdah, 32:7-9

Has not He the power to give life to the dead?
al-Qiyāmah, 75:40

Ye shall surely travel from stage to stage.
al-Inshiqāq, 84:19

The statements of the Qur'an quoted above and similar statements therein have stimulated the formulation of several theories touching the evolution of man and his destiny. But it is the biological character of these statements which has attracted special attention. Tracing the interest Muslim thinkers have evinced in the subject, Sir Muḥammad Iqbāl concentrates on the attitude assumed by the mystic poet, Jalāluddīn Rūmī and observes by way of endorsement:

"It was only natural and perfectly consistent with the spirit of the Qur'an, that Rūmī regarded the question of immortality as one of biological evolution, and not a problem to be decided by arguments of a purely metaphysical nature, as some philosophers of Islam had thought. The theory of evolution, however, has brought despair and anxiety, instead of hope and enthusiasim for life to the modern world. The reason is to be found in the unwarranted modern assumption that man's present structure, mental as well as physiological, is the last word in biological evolution, and that death, regarded as a biological event, has no constructive meaning. The world of today needs a Rūmī to create an attitude of hope, and to kindle the fire of enthusiasm for life. His inimitable lines may be quoted here:

'First man appeared in the class of inorganic things,
Next he passed there from into that of plants,
For years ye lived as one of the plants,
Remembering naught of his inorganic state so different;
And when he passed from the vegetive to the animal state,
He had no remembrance of his state as a plant,

Life Hereafter

Except the inclination he felt to the world of plants,
Especially at the time of spring and sweet flowers;
Like the inclination of infants towards their mothers,
Who know not the cause of their inclination to the breast.
Again the great Creator, as you know,
Drew man out of the animal into the human state.
Thus man passed from one order of nature to another,
Till he became wise and knowing and strong as he is now,
Of his first souls he has now no remembrance,
And he will be again changed from his present soul'".[12]

Interesting and attractive as is the vision of the evolution of man presented to us by Rūmī and endorsed in scientific terminology by Sir Muhammad Iqbāl who claims to be the disciple of *"Pir-e-Rumi"*, the point should not be overlooked that the primary purpose of the Qur'an is not to present to the world of man a factual account of the rise and development of man as might be endorsed by the discoveries of science. The statements of the Qur'an touching the subject do lend themselves to biological interpretation; but they certainly do not substantiate the view advanced by Rūmī that before man assumed his present form he had to live in succession as an inorganic substance, a plant, and an animal, or that he would replace his present form by that of an angel and so forth. Evidently he was influenced by Ibn Maskwaih (d. 421 AH) who in his *Fawz al-Akbar* equally inspired by the same Qur'anic statements has enunciated a theory

---

[12] *The Reconstruction of Religious Thought in Islam, op. cit.*, p. 114. Choudhri Ghulam Ahmad Parvez, a leading exponent of Dr. Iqbal elaborates this view in his *Ma'ārif al-Qur'ān*, vol. II, Delhi, pp. 6-29.

of the origin of man forstalling the modern scientific view. The Qur'an does postulate that man is the result of an evolutionary process and that this process will continue even after what is called death, but does not posit or specify any distinct progressive stages therein such as specified by Rūmī.

The Qur'an divides the movement into two broad periods. Firstly, there is the period when man is fashioned and receives consciousness, or to use the language of the Qur'an "has the breath of God breathed into him". This is the period which the Qur'an refers to in the verse: "It is He That has created you in diverse stages" (*Nūh*, 71:14). The period beginning with this moment and continuing thereafter crossing the line of what is termed 'death' is the second period in the life of man. It is that which the Qur'an has in view when it asserts: "Ye shall surely travel from stage to stage". The entire movement may have a biological character. But the purpose of reference to it by the Qur'an is essentially ethical and it is that which has to be kept here in view. It is to emphasise that even as from a lower stage to a higher stage man's development has been marked in the process of his making, even so, thenceforward the movement upward has to continue. Only in this latter stage the upward motion has to assume the character of a conscious movement.

During the early period no responsibility is attached to man in the making, because he is not conscious of the movement. The question of responsibility arises the moment consciousness begins to be at play. The first stage in this period which closes with what is called 'death' is the basic stage of preparation for all subsequent stages. It is the stage of freedom of will and action or of willing cooperation with the laws of life "helped by the balance set in the nature of man". What follows is but a continuation of it: "your creation and resurrection are but like a single soul". Even in this stage, the march onward is conditioned by a conscious effort appropriate to every new move. This is implicit in the urge one will feel there for Light and more and more of it. "Our Lord! Perfect our Light for us" (*al-Taḥrīm*, 66:8), will be the perennial prayer of the aspirant. Every fresh instalment of light acquired or vouchsafed is thus a new state of life accompanied by death, that necessary concomitant of life, the birth pang ushering in a new state of existence.

We have decreed Death to be your common lot.

al-Wāqi'ah, 56:60

Blessed be He in Whose hands is Dominion; and He over all things hath Power. He Who created Death and Life, that He may try which of you is best in deed.

al-Mulk, 67:1-2

Throughout, the ethical purpose persists. It is this aspect, the ethical, which the Qur'an desires to emphasise for the guidance of man, and not exactly the biological. That this aspect has not been lost sight of by Rūmī not withstanding his biological obsession as displayed in his lines quoted by Sir Muḥammad Iqbāl, is clear from a re-statement of the same biological process in the following lines:

"I died as a mineral and became a plant,
I died as plant and rose to animal,
I died as animal and I was man.
Why should I fear? When was I less by dying?
Yet once more I shall die as man, to soar,

With angels blest; but even from angelhood
I must pass on: all except God doth perish
When I have *sacrificed* my angel-soul,
I shall become what no mind e'er conceived.
Oh, let me not exist! for Non-existence
Proclaims in organ tones: 'To Him we shall return'".[13]

Here the biological process, even as Rūmī conceives, is rendered dependent upon a conscious effort, upon the 'sacrifice' of a lower nature in search of a higher.

How to discard or sacrifice in this present life the lower nature in search of a higher, or, to secure in this very life the privilege of an easy movement in the next, is the question which presents itself for consideration. The answer is already given by the Qur'an: "Believe and work righteously". But what is righteous work as warranted by a belief in the 'life-hereafter'".

It may be recalled that the Qur'an assigns to man "the vicegerency of God on earth". Be it noted that the term is not repeated or applied to him in relation to his life hereafter. The reason is obvious. The belief in the unity of God and in the truth of the divine message delivered from time to time through His messengers is to express itself in the unity of man, or in a peaceful order of existence for him. The function of Vicegerency has a meaning only in relation to this specific purpose. It ceases with death, for the character of life hereafter assumes a change. It has no longer the same sociological or economic or political background for the display of its activity. There, God does not

---

13 Rūmī, *Selections* by R. Nicholson, p. 103.

Life Hereafter

need to speak to man through "inspiration, or from behind a veil, or by the sending of a messenger" (*al-Shūrā*, 42:51). On the other hand, he comes face to face with Reality and finds his own way guided by whatever light his past existence might throw before him, intensified by further light vouchsafed to him, as a recompense, in his new surroundings. There, neither the wealth nor the power of the past will avail. There will be there little talk of democracies or parliaments, or elections or of any schemes of world security. The most powerful and exalted in this life who have lived unrighteous lives may have to step aside to let their own erstwhile valets, who have lived righteous lives, pass by in their onward march. "Those who were blind in this world, will be blind in the Hereafter", says the Qur'an, "and most astray from the Path" (*al-Isrā'*, 17:72). It is this road that matters. The Qur'an desires man to enter on this road in this world itself, so that he may equip himself with the requisite talent to have a freer passage thereon when he resumes or pursues it in the next. "What is the life of this world but amusement and play?", adds the Qur'an, "but verily the Home in the Hereafter—that is life indeed" (*al-'Ankabūt*, 29:64). This "life indeed" is to begin in this world itself.

The "life indeed" is marked by an yearning on the part of the traveller in the next for light and more of light. "Perfect for us, O Lord, our light" will be according to the Qur'an his constant prayer—the light that must lead him on into the very presence of Reality, "the countenance of God", the very "Light of the Heavens and of the Earth", as the Qur'an terms it.

> *God is the Light of the heavens and the earth. The Parable of His Light is as if there were a Niche and within it a*

Lamp: the Lamp enclosed in Glass: the glass as it were a brilliant star: lit from a blessed Tree, an Olive, neither of the East nor of the West, whose oil is well-nigh luminous, though fire scarce touched it: Light upon Light! God doth guide whom He will to His light.

al-Nūr, 24:35

The yearning for light has to begin in this life; and this is possible only for those who feel what is called "*huzur al-qalb*" or "the sense of God" in every situation. Prayed the Prophet in a moment of ecstacy:

"O Allah pour light into my heart Pour it into my eyes, and into my ears. Pour it to my right and pour it to my left. Pour it in front of me and behind me and give me light. Pour light into my nerves and into my flesh, and into my blood, and into my hair and into my skin, and into my tongue and into my soul and increase my light, and transform me into light, and surround me with light. O Allah, Bless me with light".[14]

The injunction "believe and work righteously" has a special meaning for one who feels the sense of God in all that he feels or does. The sense of God marks the difference between those who do a thing because it has to be done, is a duty imposed, because it brings them reward or because it has to be done to avoid discomfort in life, between these and those who do a thing not exactly for the recompense that it may bring, but because a good deed, however trying in its accomplishment, is good in

---

14 *Concept of Society in Islam, op. cit.*, p. 74.

Life Hereafter

itself and is pleasing to God, a thought in which he finds comfort and peace of mind. It is this sense that marked, though in a restricted sphere, the life of the Negro boy introduced in our opening chapter which one has to develop here if one is to equip oneself for the onward march from state to state in the next sphere of existence. To such men or women Paradise has no abiding attraction. Like that great sage of Baghdad, Shaykh ʻAbdul Qādir al-Jaylānī, they aspire to leave Paradise behind once they reach it and march onward beyond it towards greater light and greater perfection.

But few may possess or develop the talent so to live the life hereafter or the "life indeed" even in their earthly environment. But no life according to the Qur'an is worthy of the name, if it does not, in one form or another, partake of this aim in life, and that is not possible unless one develops, in some degree or other, the sense of God that we have spoken of, a sense which develops and thrives in inverse proportion to the elimination or subjugation of the sense of 'self' with which man is usually obsessed.

Total elimination of the sense of 'self' is not, however, the standard of conduct recommended by the Qur'an for the generality of mankind. That is the urge of a certain type of mind which seeks for its bliss "absorption in God" or *fanā fī Allāh*, to use a Ṣūfī term. No one may deny one the privilege of such an urge. But the experience, mystic as it must be, of the absorption in God is of value to society only to the extent it transmutes itself into an idea as we have observed in a previous chapter, such as may have a social or spiritual value for mankind. What the Qur'an desires man to achieve is not the total forgetefulness of his sense of the self but a happy blending of it with the sense of God in him, or the keeping of an even balance between the two. That is *taqwā* or balanced life. It is that which characterizes the mind al-Qur'an builds, a mind which looks upon life as a gift from God, as a trust and a sacred privilege to be lived in the presence of the 'Divine Countenance', and guided by the light emanating therefrom, indeed transformed into light, so that one might be an example and guide to those struggling in darkness.

CHAPTER 7
Ummatun Wasaṭ

IN THE preceding pages an attempt has been made to afford a bird's-eye view of the type of mind which it is the purpose of the Qur'an to evolve—a mind which gives to the world its *ṣālihīn* and *muttaqīn*, its *muqsitīn* and *muflihīn*, its *ṣādiqīn* and *ṣiddīqīn*, and the rest of the order referred to already, who live and work in full consciousness of the sense of God developed in them. It is to a band of people with a mind so moulded—the comrades or companions of the Prophet, and those who followed in their footsteps that the Qur'an addresses the appellation *ummatun wasaṭ* a community standing midway between two extremes, or living a balanced life, and serving as "witnesses over the nations, and the Messenger a witness over yourselves" (*al-Baqarah*, 2:143). The term but denotes the character which this mind has to assume on the organizational or corporate plane.

It was this *ummatun wasaṭ* which the Prophet organized into a state, the very first state in Islam, an organization which was intended to serve in the fullness of time as a nucleus of a world order. When we say that the Prophet organized his people into a state, we mean that he had time only to lay the foundations of it by giving them the sense of unity which they needed, leaving the task of raising the edifice thereon to posterity. His primary or immediate concern was to develop the personality of the individual and equip him with the talent to live in peace with himself and in peace with his external world of relations. And this, he did in the sure confidence that with the creation of the right type of men and women, a political structure appropriate to the corporate living of such individuals would evolve itself on right lines as a matter of course.

From the circumstances of its birth and its early nourishment, it is by no means easy to designate this state by any one of the terms applied to the different forms of government known to history. It was certainly not theocracy; for here, there was no sacerdotal caste to exercise political authority under the immediate direction of God, a form of government which prevailed particularly among the Israelites till the time of Saul. The Qur'an cannot countenance sacerdotalism in any form. The nascent state left behind by the Prophet did undoubtedly develop during the regimes of the first round of Caliphs, the '*Rāshidūn*', certain distinct qualities foreshadowing in practice the leading aspects of a thorough-going political and economic democracy, but in its theoretic approach to its democratic method of government, it would not accept the basic postulate of modern democracy that the sovereignty of a state vested in its people. The Qur'an proclaims that all sovereignty belongs to God and to God alone (*al-Baqarah*, 2:107). For that same reason, the new state could not be styled kingship either, much less a dictatorship, for, neither the Prophet nor the Caliphs (*Rāshidūn*) would assume a title specifically reserved for God, or claim the right to dictate. The Prophet had simply to follow, even as every other member of the organization, the regulations revealed to him from time to time, or as suggested themselves to him in consultation with his companions (*Āli 'Imrān*, 3:159). The same attitude was observed by the *Rāshidūn*, although in their attempt to deal with new situations not covered specifically by either the Qur'anic regulations or the practice of the Prophet, they made a free use of the principle of consultation favoured of the Qur'an, of regulating their affairs by "counsel among themselves". The principle is styled *ijtihād*. The body of people consulted by them, the *shūrā*, were men of known integrity and experience enjoying the confidence of the people, the *ijmā'*.

How then are we to designate a state whose function was to maintain by democratic methods the supremacy of law, the basic part of which as laid down in the Qur'an was regarded as divinely ordained? The answer is to be sought in the specific purpose which this basic part of the State law had to serve. From its very nature, it was there essentially to supply a distinctive cultural background or a spiritual tone, to the corporate life of the *ummah* or the Muslim community. It was against this ideological background that all secular affairs were to be regulated, not by any theocratic machinery, but by counsel among its members. The form given to the new state was no doubt that of a democracy, but it was a democracy clearly distinguishable in its outlook and responsibility from the earlier types, the Athenian and the Roman, designed primarily in the interests of privileged classes. The voice of the 'demos' composing the republic of Athens, for instance, had its counterpart in the *ijmā'* or consensus of opinion among those who formed the Arabian republic. The difference lay in the sense of responsibility with which the voice of the people was exercised and the administration of the state was carried on. The responsibility of the people of the Arabian republic in giving their assent to any act of administration was in the first instance no doubt to themselves as in Athens, but it was to be coloured and directed by their sense of an ultimate responsibility to a higher power than themselves *viz.*, God, the true Sovereign of their state. That sense had to govern the conduct of the *shūrā* or the body of the Caliph's counsellors, and the conduct of the Caliph himself, as of every officer of the state appointed by him in every department of administration.

The new republic of Arabia was thus a republic of God, fearing people and its administration was carried on, in accordance with the Qur'anic notions of justice and equity, by a band of *ṣāliḥīn*, by men of known upright character affording the fullest opportunity to every citizen to live an upright life. The mere fact that the background against which this republican life was sustained is traceable to the teachings of a religion cannot justify its being designated as a religious state or theocracy. In fact no state, however professedly secular, can endure without some sort of an ethical or spiritual background to its activity. Only, it has to keep the distinction clear between the principles which form the background and the manner and method of putting them into execution. The latter is essentially a secular function, whereas the former is there to give a particular cultural or moral tone to it. The distinction is implicit in the Qur'anic view of life which divides its function into *ḥuqūq Allāh* and *ḥuqūq an-nās* or *ḥuqūq al-'ibād*, 'obligations to God', and 'obligations to Society'. The former, *ḥuqūq Allāh*, such as beliefs, prayers, and the need for purity of mind and body are primarily personal concerns of the individual, unless a deliberate public disregard of them should prove a source of nuisance to others. The latter, *huqūq an-nās* or obligations to society, on the other hand, form the essential jurisdiction of the state. These relate largely to secular affairs and secular relationships between man and man and have naturally to be regulated by secular means or methods of administration. The *Rāshidūn* in view of the nascent stage through which the *ummah* had to pass did keep a mild form of patriarchal watch on the observance of the *huqūq Allāh* and whenever necessary even, interpreted them in their application to new conditions of life in consultation with their compeers. But this by no means constituted their office into a spiritual headship of the community. The *huqūq Allāh* and *huqūq an-nās* were binding on the Caliph as they were on an other members of society, the approach to the one reflecting itself in the approach to the other.

Mark the view which Abū Bakr took of his office as the first Caliph of the new state. Said he in his very first address to his people:

"You have made me your leader, although I am in no way superior to you. Cooperate with me when I go right; correct me when I err; obey me so long as I follow the commandments of God and His Prophet; but turn away from me when I deviate."[1]

It was an experiment in democracy which the first Caliph here promises to embark upon inspired by an ever present sense

---

1 Tabarī, Ibn Jarīr al-, *Tārīkh al-Rusul wa al-Mulūk,* ed. Muhammad Abū al-Fadl Ibrāhīm, Cairo: Dār al-Ma'ārif, 1977, vol. 3, p.244; Ibn Hishām: *al-Sīrah al-Nabawiyyah*, ed. Mustafā al-Saqqā *et. al.*, Beirut/Damascus: Dār al-Khayr, 1417/1996, vol. 4, p. 232.

of God in him. But he died within three years of his accession to the *Khilāfah*. His work was taken up by 'Umar and energetically pursued. But even he had not many years to give to the experiment. He was assassinated by a migrant from Persia in the 10th year of his regime. After him came 'Uthmān followed by 'Alī both of whom were assassinated in turn apparently as a sequence to partizan rivalry. It is these first four Caliphs who are styled the '*Rāshidūn*', the rightly guided. The period covered by their *Khilāfah* does not occupy more than thirty years. It is this period which may properly be called the period of democratic experiment in Islamic polity, the spirit underlying it rising to a climax in the time of 'Umar and reaching its final subsidence in the assassination of 'Alī.

The state was regarded by the *Rāshidūn* as the state of the people, and was run for the benefit of the people as a whole. No one had any special privilege attached to his person. The Caliph was at best the first among equals; so much so, that when food and cloth had to be rationed in Madīnah, he had but to receive his share just as an ordinary citizen. Every man and every woman had the right to question him on any matter touching the state affairs. No one was above the law. 'Umar had once to appear before a subordinate judge appointed by him to answer a charge. Similarly, 'Alī had to plead a case of his against a Jew, and it was the Jew who was awarded the decree. The economic system of life formulated by the Qur'an laying a special emphasis on the uplift of the economically depressed under which a special levy was to be collected from the rich for the relief of the poor, was rigidly enforced by the state. The exchequer of the state was considered the treasury of the people, the surplus, if any, accruing at the end of a year going back to the people in the form of annuities distributed on the basis of individual needs. The Qur'anic injunctions governing the status of women as independent economic units functioning in there own individual rights were scrupulously respected and upheld.

Security of life and of property, and freedom of concience were guaranteed to non-Muslim minorities who we styled *dhimmī*, 'the protected of God and the Prophet'. "Beware! on the day of judgement," had the Prophet proclaimed, "I shall myself be the complainant against him who wrongs a *dhimmī* or lays on him a responsibility greater than he can bear or deprives him of anything that belongs to him".[2] Indeed, so mindful was he of their welfare that a few moments before he expired, the thought of the *dhimmī* came to him. He said: "Any Muslim who kills a *dhimmī* has not the slightest chance of catching even the faintest smell of Heaven. Protect them: They are any *dhimmī*". In a moment of like remembrance, 'Umar as he lay assassinated, exclaimed: "To him who will be Caliph after me, I commend my wish and testament! The *dhimmī* are protected of Allah and the Prophet. Respect the covenants entered into with them, and when necessary fight for their interests, and do not place on them, a burden or responsibility which they cannot bear".

"When Jerusalem submitted to the Caliph 'Umar", states Sir Thomas Arnold in *The Preaching of Islam*, "the following conditions were drawn up:

'In the name of God, the merciful, the compassionate, the following are the terms of capitulation, which I, 'Umar, the

---

2 Al-Māwardī: *al-Aḥkām as-Sulṭāniyyah*, Cairo, Ch. XIII, p. 137.

servant of God, the Commander of the Faithful, grant to the people of Jerusalem. I grant them security of lives, their possessions, and their children, their churches, their crosses, and all that appertains to them in their integrity, and their lands and to all, of their religion. their churches therein shall not be impoverished, nor destroyed, nor injured from among them; neither their endowments, nor their dignity; and not a thing of their properly; neither shall the inhabitants of Jerusalem be exposed to violence in following their religion; nor shall one of them be injured'".[3]

Adds Arnold:
"In company with the Patriarch, 'Umar visited the holy places and it is said while they were in the Church of the Resurrection, as it was the appointed hour of prayer, the Patriarch bade the Caliph offer his prayers there, but he thoughtfully refused, saying that if he were to do so, his followers might afterwards claim it as a place of Muslim worship".[4]

In the conduct of war, even as in the other spheres of activity, the *Rāshidūn* never lost sight of humanitarian considerations enjoined by the Qur'an. "The self-restraint of the conquerors and the humanity which they displayed in their campaigns", observes Arnold, "must have excited profound respect and secured a welcome for an invading army that was guided by such principles of justice and moderation as were laid down by the Caliph Abū Bakr for the guidance of the first

---

3 Sir Thomas Arnold: *The Preaching of Islam*, p. 51.

4 Ibid. p. 51.

expedition into Syria:

> 'Be just; break not your plighted Faith; mutilate none; slay neither children, old men nor women; injure not the date palm nor burn it with fire, nor cut down any fruit, bearing tree; slay neither flocks nor herds nor camels, except for food; perchance you may come across a men who have retired into monastries, leave them and their works in peace'".[5]

The democracy of the *Rāshidūn* which certainly displayed in that dark period of human history qualities such as these of a model state, *'ummatun wasaṯ'* might have grown by now, had it had a free life, into a veritable 'fold' of the Prophet's vision, indeed developed into a world federation of autonomous communities, every constituent member whereof being a "shephard or keeper unto every other". But that was not to be. The tragedy of Islam is that this tender plant was not allowed to grow. It was cut down by the hands of its own followers within a few years of the passing away of the Prophet, and replaced in the very name of that Faith by varying forms of despotism. But while it lasted, however brief the period of its existence, it functioned, at least during its brilliant moments, consciously as an *ummatun wasaṯ*.

The *'ulamā* or doctors of religion of the present day refer to the Prophetic regime as *ḥukm ilāhī* or divine governance or theocracy. They extend its application to the regime of the *Rāshidūn* Caliphs as well, although the circumstances of the time of the *Rāshidūn* were not precisely the same as of that of the Prophet. They go a step further. The *Rāshidūn* had to follow the

---

[5] Ibid. pp. 49-50.

commandments as laid down in the Qur'an in the light of the practice or *Sunnah* of the Prophet as personally or directly known to them being themselves the Prophet's companions. That was their approach to the basic law of Islam. But our *'ulamā'* will apply the term to what was devised after the *Rāshidūn* by the legists of the second and third centuries of the Hijrah, on the basis, on the one hand, of the hearsay or oral Prophetic tradition and of the practice of the *Rāshidūn*, and on the other of interpretations placed on the text of the Qur'anic injunctions by the exigetists of the times.

This form of law is called *fiqh* and is divided into several schools or *madhāhib*, each secure in its role as the infallible and unalterable law of Islam. The curious feature of this output is that while it is itself in many respects the result of *ijtihād* on the part of its framers, it is interpreted to deny the exercise of this privilege to those coming after them, notwithstanding the fundamental directive of the Qur'an to regulate their affairs by "counsel among themselves". At least that is so in the major spheres of life. It is this law called *sharī'ah*, as formulated by the medieval legists, which is the law of Islam for our *'ulamā'* and which they desire every Muslim State to revive and enforce at the present day.

In its resuscitated condition, this *hukm ilāhī* or divine governance is intended to take a form under which, since God does not choose to appear before man in any visible form to regulate human affairs, the voice of the *'ulamā'* who assign to themselves the sole right to interpret divine law of *sharī'ah*, shall finally prevail. Such a government clearly will be class dictatorship very much like the dictatorship of the secredotal order under the Israelite form of theocracy and should be regarded as repugnant to the spirit and purpose of the Qur'an.

As a concession, on the one hand, to the theocratic concept of government sponsored by the *'ulamā'* and, on the other, as an yielding to the pressure of the democratic idea of the present day, a tendency is aserting itself in several parts of the Muslim world to resuscitate the form of democracy tried by the *Rāshidūn*. But is that possible without reviving at the same time the atmosphere of the time of the *Rāshidūn*, vanished long since, wherein alone the Rāshidūnian form might thrive. And even if it were possible, could it comfortably fit into the world atmosphere of today? That would be pushing life 1,300 years back and living in which again is not possible. This apart, be it remembered that the *Rāshidūn* and their counsellors were men who had lived with the Prophet and had a direct or personal knowledge of the Prophetic tradition or of how and in what spirit he regulated the secular affairs of his people and gave them the character of an *ummatun wasat*. But how to reach that knowledge at this distant hour or have a clear vision of it without lifting the medieval shroud that rests thereon? In other words, are we of the present times prepared to erase from our memory all that is un-Qur'anic which we have inherited from our past with its early civil wars, its theological schizms, its autocracy and feudalism and the rest of its blemished features and rediscover for ourselves the Islam of the Prophet and the exact Rāshidūnian form which rested thereon? That will call for a bold investigation into the character and content of our traditional sources of theological knowledge, and of the early history of Islam.

The investigation is necessary whatever the purpose for

which it may be employed. The Rāshidūnian form, when discovered will have to be given a shape such as it might have assumed today, had it had a natural development undisturbed by the disturbances to which it succumbed before it could begin to live a full life. Else, we shall be reverting to a state of life that might not well fit into the present setup of the world. We shall have to re-orientate the primary attitudes of Islam in the context of the present day needs of the world; and this is not possible without clearing the debris that has blocked the view.

The task is by no means easy. It is indeed a task conjointly to be undertaken by competent scholars drawn from all over the world who may have the courage to apply the historic and scientific methods to the exegeses of the Qur'an and the literature on *ḥadīth* and *fiqh* and sift the purely *sunnat al-'Arab* or the customary law of the Arabs as has found its way into *fiqh* from the *sunnat Allāh* as actually implemented by the Prophet in the circumstances of his times, sift the genuinely Prophetic tradition from the seemingly so forged by rival political parties and warring sects of the first two centuries of the Hijrah in defence of their jarring claims and conveniently foisted on the Prophet, and at the same time sift the temporarily expedient from the lasting or universal in application. It is only then that we may have a full and clear picture of the organizational life, of the *ummatun wasaṭ* as raised by the Prophet.

The task will not end there. The restoration of the original picture or of the re-discovery of the Islam of the Prophet will be the right hour for a proper re-orientation of the Islamic thought in terms of the complex needs of the modern world. For, without this prior restoration, every attempt at re-orientation will be but a patch-work as was the case with every attempt at *ijtihād* made so far, whether in the distant past or in recent times. The stumbling block in the way has always been the dross that has been allowed to cling to the gold in the *ḥadīth* literature. Much of this is Judaic, Magian, Nestorian, or Neo-platonic in origin wilfully attributed to the Prophet giving rise to beliefs and practices so alien to the essential spirit of the Qur'an. Until the gold is sifted from that which is foreign to it and a single authorized corpus of *ḥadīth* literature and an equally authorized exegesis of the Qur'an are prepared by the joint efforts of competent scholars enjoying the requisite confidence of at least the governments of independent Muslim countries, an attempt at re-orientation of the Islamic religious, thought and codification of a common basic *fiqh* for the entire *ummah* is not likely to produce the desired result.

Till such a concerted attempt is made to rescue Islam from its medieval bondage and to re-order Muslim society everywhere on a unitary or common cultural basis, the least that may be expected of Muslims in every country, if they are to absorb the shocks of today and survive, is to develop the sense of God or the sense of humanity in all their thought and activity and cooperate on that basis with all the progressive trends of the present day world. Indeed if they are to be guided by the spirit of the Qur'an, they will have to seize these trends, and give them the Qur'anic touch which they apparently lack. For it is the lack of it that has converted these otherwise progressive trends into engines of destruction and brought about two hideous world wars in our own life-time, and look like inflicting a deadlier wound on mankind in no distant future, if that touch is not restored to them in proper time. After all, these trends, whatever their immediate stimuli, or the purposes to which they are employed by different nations in different regions of the world, are in consonance with the essential spirit of the Qur'an and indeed traceable for certain stages in their historic progress directly to its teachings.

Let the Muslims reflect. The world is marching, towards a democratic order of life for all mankind—a purpose so dear to the Qur'an. It has begun, notwithstanding the impediments blocking the way, to socialize the good things of the earth—another purpose sponsored by the Qur'an. The world of science is unraveling for man the hidden forces of nature with intensive avidity and pressing them into his service—a crying call issuing forth and reverberating from every corner of the Qur'an. There should, therefore, be no difficulty for Muslim countries in falling into line with leading trends of the modern world. Should they do so with little reference to their spiritual moorings or just to advance their own interests unmindful of the world purpose of the Qur'an, the well-being of all humanity, they will go the way the rest of the world are going and share the consequences. If, on the other hand, they should cultivate on the group plane, the sense of God on which the Qur'an lays its supreme stress as the mainspring of all life sustaining activity, even as they have to do on, the individual plane, in other words, lay even emphasis on the *huqūq Allāh* and *huqūq an-nās*, on the obligations to themselves and obligations to mankind, they may still develop into an *ummatun wasaṭ*, and serve is a balancing factor between the exaggerated opposites of the world of today.

CHAPTER 8
The Cultural Basis of Civilization[1]

"All creation is the family of God. Those are the best loved of Him who serve best His family"—*Hadīth*.[2]

In dealing with the subject I shall avoid as far as possible abstract reasoning and technical terminology, and even un-familiar names, and shall besides concentrate my attention on the fundamental basis on which a lasting culture rests and without which no culture, however dazzling, has an abiding value to the moral and material well-being of mankind at large.

The term 'culture' has been defined variously. Some have identified it with one or other of its several aspects of manifestation. Some have laid undue emphasis on only a few of the ingredients which compose it to the neglect of other ingredients; whereas some definitions have confused the term 'culture' with the term 'civilization'. I do not propose to dwell

---

1 From a chapter in Syed Abdul Latif: *Islamic Cultural Studies*, Lahore: SH Muhammad Ashraf, 1969.

2 See note 1, p. vii.

on any of these cut and dried definitions; for that will not likely help easy understanding. I would rather follow a much simpler method to know what that term really means or ought to mean. And that method is to appeal directly to common sense—the etymological sense of the word itself.

Etymologically, the word means "cultivation of the human mind or its improvement by training". Culture, in this sense, is the name for the activity of the mind, for its manifestation in all the things of life with which it is concerned. The mind is thus the mainspring of culture; and it follows that as the mind is, so its expression or the culture which it generates or throws out or shapes. Culture in this way becomes synonymous with life itself, whether that life be of an individual or of the class or group to which he belongs. In its group aspect, it marks a distinct attitude, common to the entire group and manifests itself in their language and literature, in their art and philosophy, in their customs, manners, laws and modes of worship. In a word, it represents their genius. It is such attitudes, the different group geniuses which distinguish one culture from another and from which flow the peculiarities and characteristics of the different nations of the earth.

Every culture, therefore, is at bottom, at its basis, an attitude of mind, a living idea, so to say, which inspires and moulds a people's life. An idea such as this is in reality an organism, and it lives or decays and dies according to the vitality which it possesses or is inherent in it. It is this vitality, this staying power for good or ill in a culture, which determines the scope and duration of its operation. The history of mankind has witnessed the rise and disappearance of countless cultures, because they had

The Cultural Basis of Civilization

not sufficient staying power, because the basis on which they rested had no abiding value to human life. On the other hand, cultures there have been though few in number, and have had a longer day or have persisted to live on through the vicissitude of time. And this, because of their greater staying power. But whatever their length of life, there is this to be observed, as a characteristic common to them all, that while they have lasted, the idea on which and for which each one of them has lived has operated as a religious, or almost a religious, force. The idea might have been a legacy of tradition, historical or mythological, or it might have been the result of reasoning or necessity or an impulse, or it might have been a part of what is called Divine Revelation. But it has been there to inspire the activity of those who have believed in it. And it is in that role that it interests us as the basis of their culture. If then, it is an idea, an ideal, an 'ism' which ultimately supplies the motive—the basis—for group activity in its different spheres, it follows that the higher the basic idea, the 'ism' which a culture embodies or reflects, the higher and the more lasting its influence on mankind. It is why cultures which have been based on certain verities of life, or have satisfied certain universal moral or spiritual laws of life, have had a longer day of influence.

In societies where this truth is not understood in its proper perspective, the term 'culture' is confused with the term 'refinement'. In this indifferent or popular sense, the term 'culture' stands for the fashion of the day, primarily in the externalia of life—in dress, in drawing-room manners, in material amenities of living and in similar signs of seeming or outward polish. But such a condition or state may likely be a veneer, a show, a pose, not necessarily arguing a refined state of mind. "One may smile and smile and yet be a villain," says Hamlet, and he draws attention to what should not pass for culture.

Before I proceed any further let me make clear to you what I mean by another term which, in the course of my present discourse, I shall have to use. It is the term 'civilization'. Even here, I am not going to worry you by a plethora of definitions advanced by the protagonists of different civilizations. I shall simply let its etymological sense, as in the case of the term 'culture', make its appeal to common sense, because, it is the commonsense view which inevitably should hold the ground.

Etymologically considered, 'civilization' should mean "perfecting of civil life or of the relations of men among themselves". It is in this sense that we arrange the order of civilizations, assigning one to an inferior position than another. The test is the quality of perfection attained; and the higher the quality, the superior the civilization. This quality is determined by two factors, or rather it is a mixture of two ingredients capable of blending into each other. One is this: if civil life is to be perfected, it must represent organized social relations based, on the one hand, on increasing production of the means of giving strength and happiness to society, and, on the other, on an equitable distribution amongst individuals of the strength and happiness so produced. This is a primary condition of civilization. There is another condition which should be fulfilled. Civilization must also represent a process of perfection of the individual himself, of his faculties, his sentiments, his ideas making organized civil life humane or such as may glorify human nature. In other words, 'civilization' must always manifest two symptoms—progress of society, and progress of humanity. A society may be fully developed and its distribution of wealth within its own circle quite equitable; but it may prove a curse to humanity at large all the same. Hence it is that we insist, in every civilization, on the presence in some degree of this second quality which makes for the progress of humanity. And the greater the degree in which this quality blends with the other quality, the higher the station it occupies among civilizations.

I may now come back to my subject. The second quality which I have just dwelt upon as being so indispensable to civilization is a cultural strain. But it is a strain which does not proceed from every culture. For, as I have already indicated, cultures have not all the same vitality, the same abiding value to humanity. Some are distinctly pernicious; some, though by no means pernicious, are yet so circumscribed in their scope of usefulness that they cannot develop that quality of universal application which can give rise to a noble civilization or sustain it. So, if a civilization is to be truly noble, truly great, it must, for its second quality, incorporate in its texture a culture whose foundations lie deep in the eternal and all-pervasive spiritual law of life which has struggled through ages to mould mankind into one entity. For it is only on such a basis of organized life, and through such a culture, that a true civilization can live and thrive.

What then is the culture which can fashion a noble civilization which in its turn can evolve a noble world order and stand surety for its sustained maintenance?

It may be recalled that a civilization worthy of its name must manifest two symptoms—progress of society and progress of humanity, the one dependent on the other. In other words, a civilization to be truly noble must represent an organized civil life inspired by a culture which stands for the progress of humanity. Where you have this, or where the two objects are served together, you have a civilization which possesses a universal value for all mankind and is a blessing to it. On the other hand, where material progress is confined to an exclusive class or section of a society or community, or where the progress, while comprehending the needs of even the entire community, depends for its sustenance on the continued exploitation of other communities, you have an organized life but no civilization. Again, where a community as a community is in the vanguard of material progress, but where the individual has no status or the individual soul is not allowed a free play but is merged or lost in an impersonal mass-soul or mass-soullessness, even here you have no civilization. Or further, where life is organized on an hierarchical basis, one layer of caste or class rising above another, each again vertically divided into innumerable sections on the basis of absolute and rigid social exclusiveness, however progressive the entire organization materially, you have not merely no civilization but a deliberate negation of it.

In none of these or similar situations will you have a civilization in the real sense of the term, because the cultural strain animating all such organized activities is not conducive to the progress of the individual and of humanity. That is the reason why

"Empire after Empire at their height of sway
Have felt this boding sense come on;
Have felt their huge frames not constructed right,
And dropped, and slowly died upon their throne."

Why did the Greek civilization, with all its glorious achievements in the realm of knowledge and thought and art and science, perish, and transmit its curse, its disease to the modern European civilization? You know the structure of the Greek city state, the city state idealized by Plato and other equally illustrious sons of Greece. Who can deny that the Greeks through their city state of Athens, for instance, have given us a highly perfected conception of democratic life, of a democracy where knowledge was free and full, where beauty both in form and thought was superb, where the mind of its citizen could reach its highest summits? We have been taught by our universities to call this civilization of the Greek city state as a noble civilization—the charm of its beautiful exterior is so irresistible to its devotees! But how many of our servants and thinkers have taken the trouble to realize adequately that under the beautiful exterior of the city state, there was stamped by its very nature a deep scar of concentrated leprosy on its soul which was eventually to be its undoing? That scar was the pariah land permanently fixed as an appendage to the city state—a portion of the city where the slave, the political untouchable, was quartered to sweat for the privileged citizen of the Greek Republic, and provide him with the material amenities of life. Living thus on the labour of the downtrodden, the philosophers of Greece complacently engaged themselves in the task of unravelling the problems of humanity! But bear this in mind. Humanity to the Greek mind meant the Hellenes, the Greeks, in contrast to the non-Greeks, styled 'Barbarians', living within and without the land of Hellos. That was the mode of classical life and thought which was transmitted to Rome only to intensify an already existing exclusive class-consciousness on which the Roman State had been raised.

This is the cultural strain which through the wreckage of the Roman Empire was transmitted to the Middle Ages and the Continental Renaissance giving rise to geographical patriotism and racial nationalism converting Europe into a network of contending rival military camps. This is the strain which exploited the Industrial Revolution to metamorphose the old feudal order of lords and guilds and pariahs into an industrial order of capitalists, the *grande bourgeoisie*, and the professional classes of technicians, and administrators, *petite-bourgeoisie*, and the working classes, the pariah *proletariat*; and this is the strain which supplied the urge to every geographical nationality in Europe, even the tiniest, to embark on colonial ventures all over the globe outside of Europe, and carve out pariah lands for themselves.

Such is the strain which originally emaciated from Greece and Rome and which has till now held under its grip the mind of the Western man. Its concentrated leprosy has brought about wars in our days. Of what value to mankind in general are the conceptions and ideals which European thinkers and administrators place before us as universally valid when, in moments of crisis, we are made to realize that their furthest horizon does not extend beyond the narrow geographical walls of their respective national homes in Europe, even as the intellectual horizon of Plato, when speaking of humanity, did not transcend the boundaries of the land of his own people, the Hellenes? Hence it is that Europe has failed to evolve a civilization such as might bring the blessings of organized material progress in equal degree to every part of the globe. It is a misnomer to call a state

The Cultural Basis of Civilization

of affairs such as this as civilization; for, while organized material progress is essential to civilization, no achievement, political, social, economic, or scientific generating strength and means of happiness, will have a universal value unless it can be measured in terms of human life.

It is said that European civilization is not all Hellenic, or Roman or Teutonic at bottom, is not all anti-pariah, and that whatever the strains which might have proceeded from these sources to shape it, they have all been kept in proper check by the universal humanitarian strain proceeding from Christianity. But is that so?

As things stand, a half of Europe where Bolshevism and Nazism prevail, Christianity has been given the go-by; and, in the remaining half, the Prince of Peace has no effective hold on the national life of his followers. The Christian evangelist throughout the course of European history has very often endeavoured not so much to establish the Kingdom of God on earth, even as Christ wished, as to enjoin on his Christian fold an un-Christian commandment foisted on Christ: "Render unto Caesar the things which are Caesar's; and unto God the things that are God's", thereby pushing the vision of the Kingdom out of sight. To speak the truth, European Christianity has, barring stray occasions subserved the interests of Caesar rather than those of God and countenanced therefore the expansion of the pariah land all over the world.

So, how is the world to evolve a civilized life for man or humanize his life? When Europe can give us no lead, when its much-vaunted civilization is afflicted with a fatal disease where are we to turn for solace and inspiration? With nerves shattered by its civilization, can we rebuild the world out of its ruins and establish the Kingdom of God therein? That is the issue which is staring us in the face today and which will stare harder tomorrow.

If mankind is to come into its own, it will have to make a supreme effort to throw off the disease to which it has clung for so long. But will it do it? Or, will it go another long round of agony? The disease is of the spirit and will call for a remedy of the spirit.

If Europe and all those countries outside of it which have imbibed its spirit are to turn over a new leaf, they must reorientate their cultural outlook and accept or return to ideas on which alone the Kingdom of God will rest and through which alone humanity will find universal peace and happiness.

I have borrowed the term 'Kingdom of God' deliberately from religious vocabulary, partly for the reason that there is no other term which can so fully express my view of a new world order, but chiefly because I am firmly convinced in mind that whatever the order one may evolve for tomorrow, it will not stand for long unless it satisfies some spiritual law of life or fulfils some high universal moral purpose, and is determined, at the same time, never to let the law of the jungle, or the pagan conception of the survival of the fittest and the control of the world by a race of supermen, raise its hideous head again to renew the struggle for the sovereignty of the earth. If humanity is not to perish in this process, it must make a joint endeavour in time to hand back the sovereignty of the earth to God; for, as the Qur'an points out, the sovereignty of, the earth and of whatsoever that there is in it belongs only to God and we are but to hold it in trust for Him as his vicegerents and jointly enjoy its wholesome goods—one standing surety for every other—and thus live in peace and happiness.

Jointly enjoy the wholesome goods of the earth! That seems to be the primary privilege and function of humanity. But the task has been neglected and we are reaping the consequence.

Mischief has appeared on land and sea because of (the meed) that the hands of men have earned, that (God) may give them a taste of some of their deeds: in order that they may turn back (from Evil).

al-Rūm, 30:41

This is the lesson of history, the eternal law of life. When man through perverseness has very nearly reached the edge of a precipice from where another step forward will assuredly end in a dreadful fall, he should pause and retrace. Will he do that? The effort will no doubt be arduous particularly for the European nations and for those who have begun to imitate them in other parts of the world. But they will have to make that effort if they cared to be saved. The hour is propitious; for never before in the history of man did the earth look like a compact house as it does today, though unfortunately the house is divided against itself; for the achievements of science have dismantled all geographical obstacles of time and space and have so quickened the means of communication that even whispers can be overheard from corner to corner. Never before was there so great an opportunity for mankind to come closer together and demonstrate that they were all 'children of God' as Christ said, or as members of one single 'family of God' as said the Prophet of Islam. Now is the time to realize that racial or exclusive nationalism is a curse to mankind, and that man as man should be allowed to feel and live as a free citizen of the world and live wherever his fancy or desire or aptitude takes him. But the effort to remodel life on that cultural basis will by no means be easy for those who have lived or aspire to live on the exploitation of the weak. But if the recent wholesale fire-baths all over the world can be regarded as a divine warning, they will have to go through the ordeal.

If the world is to be reconstituted on any abiding basis, the first thing that needs to be effected is the liberation of subject countries and the emancipation of subject peoples. As a corollary to this, it will be necessary to abolish caste and pariah systems wherever and in whatever form they exist, and to democratize social life in every community. If that were done, we shall have the world peopled by free communities, free to combine on a world basis for their mutual good.

CHAPTER 9
Prayers in Islam[1]

TO UNDERSTAND the spirit of a religion, and appraise its value to life and society, read the prayers which its followers generally employ in their communion with God. They will afford an insight into the working of their minds, their thoughts and feelings, and the very objects of their lives. There is no prevarication, no hiding or suppression of truth, no luxurious display of poetic fancy when man stands face to face with the Creator of his being to lay bare before Him his heart, and give account of his mundane struggles, his achievements and disappointments, and to ask of Him the things that matter. His prayer, at such a moment, is an expression of a pressing feeling, and is for that reason naturally simple and direct. The higher the note that he strikes in his outpourings, the higher is the quality of the faith that has imprinted itself on his mind, and served as a background to all his activity.

In Islam, the prayer that a Muslim offers whether singly, or in congregation, whether at the appointed hours of devotion, or at any sudden call or urge from within to turn to his Lord in the

---

1 From a chapter in Syed Abdul Latif: *Islamic Cultural Studies*, Lahore: SH Muhammad Ashraf, 1969.

midst of his daily work, is all couched in the phraseology of the Qur'an or that of the Prophet's own utterances preserved in the *aḥādīth*. Even when the suppliant expresses himself in his own tongue, the form of prayer is dictated by the same sources. The same attitude towards his Master, the same conception behind the words used, the same spiritual atmosphere generated by them are revived in his mind, and nothing that he says is not covered by the teachings of his holy Scripture and the example of his holy Prophet:

> "O Allah! I ask of Thee the good that Thy servant and Prophet had asked for himself; and seek Thy refuge from the evil wherefrom Thy servant and Prophet had sought refuge".[2]

is the prayer that opens for a Muslim an endless prospect of sublime aspirations. For, what might not the great exemplar have asked of his Lord, the Creator and Sustainer of all things, to Whom alone belongeth the Kingdom, from Whom alone cometh every strength, Whose knowledge encompasseth all, and Whose power suffused with love dwelleth everywhere. In a note such as this, it may seem out of place to refer to the utterances of the Prophet having mystic significance, utterances which reflect the most exalted moods wherein he found himself in moments of the closest communion with Allah, the Holy, the Pure, Whom he loved and worshipped with an intensity such as he alone did experience. To but few is given that experience and that state of mind wherein one may ask of the things that the Prophet had asked for himself. Let us therefore deal with only such prayers

---

2 Editor's note: The author has liberally quoted in this chapter excerpts of the Prophet's prayers from *aḥādīth*, some sources of which we have given in the footnotes.

Prayers in Islam 125

of the Prophet as put in mind the aspirations that need to be entertained so as to live a life of purity and social service, a life which is within the reach of everyone who may strive or ask for it.

"O Allah! make Islam most pleasing to me", is one of the prayers included here. It is a brief utterance; yet, how superbly comprehensive! The suppliant here asks for the path of Islam to be smoothed down for him, to be made most pleasing—the path of Islam, which is truly the path of devotion, of bringing our own will into accord with the Supreme will, or of devoting all our talents to the service of the highest in life. He asks for a life disciplined in the ways of Allah or the laws intrinsic in our nature. It is a duty, in the discharge of which few there are who can claim not to have faltered. Yet, a true Muslim is to ask of God to make such a task most pleasing to him.

It is towards this end that every prayer of Islam is directed. Mark the character of the following two prayers which have found their way into the regular daily worship of a, Muslim. One is the common prayer of Islam and the most compulsory with which every service begins, an the other is what enters into his vespers:

> *All praise is due to Allah, the Lord of the worlds, the Beneficent, the Merciful; Master of the Day of Judgment! Thee do we worship, and of Thee do we seek help. Show us the right path, the path of those whom Thou hast blessed, and not of those whom Thou hast shown Thy disapprobation, nor of those who have gone astray.*
>
> al-Fatiḥah, 1:1-7

This prayer serves as a recurrent reminder to a Muslim of the character of life that he is to pursue—a life of purity, and of righteous conduct. The same note is struck in the vespers:

> O Allah! guide me to be of those whom Thou hast guided and preserve me to be of those whom Thou hast preserved and befriend me to be of those whom Thou hast befriended, and bless me in what Thou dost grant me, and protect me from the evil of everything that Thou mayest prescribe for me: for, surely, Thou alone canst prescribe what Thou desireth, and none can overrule Thee. Surely, he whom Thou befriendest is not disgraced. Blessed art Thou, our Lord, and Exalted![3]

Note the spirit of the following prayer:

> O Allah! improve my spiritual for that is to be my refuge; and improve my material life, for I have to live it; and prepare me for the life to which I shall have to return; and keep me alive till it is good for me to be alive, and call me back when it is good for me to die. Lengthen my life in every goodly state, and turn death into bliss before any evil state supervenes.[4]

Death has thus no terror for a Muslim. The thing that he should fear and abhor is wickedness or evil life; and it is against this that he has to seek the Divine help and protection. In whatever he may ask for, he is never to forget his primary need for purity of life.

O Allah! I ask of Thee a pure life and a pure death, and a

---

3 *Sunan al-Tirmidhī*, "Kitāb al-Salāt", *hadīth* No. 426; *Sunan al-Nasā'ī*, "Kitāb Qiyām al-Layl wa Tadāwwu' al-Nahār", *hadīth* Nos. 1725-1726.

4 *Sahīh Muslim*, "Kitāb al-Dhikr wa al-Du'ā", *hadīth* No. 4897.

returning unto Thee that shall not call for reprehension or disgrace.

O Allah! keep Thou me steady, and add weight to my work; confirm me in my faith, and raise me in Thy regard, and accept my worship, and shield me from sins and bless me with high places in heaven. Amen!

O Allah! I am truly weak; turn my weakness into strength that I may follow Thy will, and draw me towards goodness; and make Islam most pleasing to me.

O Allah! I beseech Thee to grant me goodness in my speech, and goodness in my thought and action, and goodness in my inward and outward aspects, and high places in heaven. Amen!

O Allah! help me to stand in Islam, to sit in Islam, and to sleep in Islam; and do not let my enemies or the jealous rejoice over my trials.

O Allah! I seek Thy refuge from the knowledge of that which brings no good, and from that mind that has no fear of God, and from that desire that cannot be satiated, and from that prayer that cannot be entertained. O Allah! I seek refuge from thee.[5]

O Allah! make every action of mine sublime in its outcome; and save me from disgrace in this world and from chastisement in the hereafter.

---

5 *Saḥīḥ Muslim*, "Kitāb al-Dhikr wa al-Duʿā", hadīth No. 4899; *Sunan al-Tirmidhī*, "Kitāb al-Daʿawāt", *hadīth* No. 3404.

Our Lord! Condemn us not if we forget or fall into error. Our Lord! Lay not on us a burden like that which Thou didst lay on those before us. Our Lord! Lay not on us a burden greater than we have strength to bear. Blot out our sins, and grant us forgiveness. Have mercy on us. Thou art our Protector; help us against those who stand against Faith.

al-Baqarah, 2:286.

O Allah! Surely, I have done great injustice to myself, and none can wipe out my sins but Thou; therefore, grant me Thy protection, and have mercy on me; surely, Thou alone art the Protector, the Merciful!

O Ever-Living Providence! I crave of Thee, through Thy grace, to correct every aspect of my life, and I pray Thee never for a moment to deliver me to my desires.

O Allah! I seek refuge from Thy disapprobation in Thy approbation, from Thy chastisement in Thy forgiveness. O Allah! I seek refuge from Thee in Thee. O Allah! I cannot sufficiently extol Thee, for, Thou alone canst extol Thyself.

O Allah! I am weak; give me strength. I am lowly, give me honour; I am indigent, give me subsistence, and create a distance between me and wickedness such as there is between the East and the West.

O Allah! I beseech Thee to let no sin of mine remain unforgiven, no worry unremoved, no debt unpaid, and no want of this or of the life coming after unsatisfied. O Thou kindest of the kind!

O Allah! There is nothing easy of achievement except what Thou so maketh: and Thou maketh the difficult easy, whensoever Thou liketh. There is no God besides Him, the Forbearing, the Magnanimous. Pure is He, the Master of the highest Throne. Praise is for Him only, the Lord of all the worlds!

I ask of Thee the qualities which move Thy grace, and forgiveness. I ask of Thee protection from doing harm to anyone, and I ask of Thee the chance of doing good to everyone.

O Allah! I seek my well-being through Thy knowledge, and my strength through Thy strength, and I ask of Thy great benevolence; for, verily, Thou art powerful, and I am powerless; I am ignorant, and Thou art Knowing; and Thou knowest all that we do not know.

In the expression of a Muslim's wishes, there can be no thought of gaining anything at the expense of another. Indeed, there is an intense regard in, his prayers for the good and welfare of everyone. The aim of his life is that it may be lived in the presence of the Divine Countenance, and guided by the light emanating therefrom, indeed transformed into light, so that he may be an example and guide to those struggling in darkness.

O Allah! I ask of Thee steadfastness in every pursuit. I ask of Thee the intent for good action, and the power to thank Thee for Thy benevolence, and to render Thee devoted service. I ask of Thee the tongue that speaketh truth and the mind that erreth not, and the gift of true fellow-feeling. I seek Thy refuge from the evil of everything that Thou knoweth; and I ask of Thee the good that lieth in everything that Thou knoweth; and I seek Thy refuge from every sin of which Thou hast knowledge. And verily Thou knoweth all that we cannot know.

O God! bring affection between us, and reform us, and open for us paths of peace, and take us out of the spheres of darkness into light, and save us from open and concealed sinfulness, and bless us in what we hear, and in what we see, and in what we feel, and bless us in our help-meets and in our children; and turn Thou to us again; for Thou only canst turn in kindness again and again.

O Allah! the good that I have received this morning, and that which the other creatures of Thine have received are all from Thee, the One besides Whom there is none, Who alone is deserving of praise and thanksgiving. O Allah! give soundness of health to my body; O Allah! give soundness of hearing to my ears; O Allah! give soundness of sight to my eyes. There is no God but Thee.[6]

O Allah! I seek Thy refuge from misleading others, and from being misled by others; from betraying others into error, and from being betrayed into error by others; from doing any wrong to others and from being wronged by others; and from drawing others into ignorance and from being drawn into ignorance by others.[7]

O Allah! bless me always with the joy of Thy sight and the pleasure of beholding Thy Countenance unharmed by anything

---

[6] *Sunan al-Tirmidhī*, "Kitāb al-Daʿawāt", *hadīth* No. 3402; *Sunan al-Nasāʾī*, "Kitāb al-Istiʿadhah", *hadīth* No. 5361.

[7] *Sunan Abi Dāwūd*, "Kitāb al-Adab", *hadīth* No. 4430.

harmful and undisturbed by anything disturbing. O Allah! I seek Thy refuge from any wrong that I may do to others, and from any wrong that others may do to me; from any harshness that I may show to others, and from any harshness that others may show to me; and from any sin that Thou mayest not forgive.

O Allah! make us guides in the path of life, and keep us guided ourselves therein,—neither going astray, nor leading astray. Keep us friendly to those who are Thy friends, and hostile to those who are hostile to Thee. We love him who loveth Thee and hate him who doth hate Thee. O Allah! this is our prayer and it is for Thee to accept it. We are but to try and trust.

O Allah! pour light into my heart, and into my eyes, and into my ears. Pour it to my right and pour it to my left. Pour it in front of me and behind me, and give me light. Pour light into my nerves, and into my flesh and into my blood, and into my hair and into my skin, and into my tongue, and into my soul, and increase my light, and transform me into light, and surround me with light. O Allah! bless me with light.

Index

abad 81, 82
Abbāsids 4, 7, 43
'Abdul Qādir al-Jaylānī,
    Shaykh 95
Abraham 16, 17
Abū Bakr 101, 105
Adam 22, 23
adultery 66
ahādīth 33, 125
a'jamī 7
Allah 31, 32, 44, 47, 50, 54,
    57, 64-73, 76, 83, 94, 95,
    100, 101, 103, 108, 111,
    125-131
    Ways of 14, 27, 46, 51,
        67, 70, 126
'Alī 16, 102
alms-giving 27
'amal sālih 26, 60
American vi
amthāl 6, 74-76
anarchy 10
Andrews, C. F. 12
animal(s) 25, 35, 89, 92
anthropomologists 14
anthropomorphic 6
ahqāb 82
Arab 6, 7, 46, 108
    community 46
    non- 6, 7
Arabia 2, 13, 44, 100
Arabian 100
    frontiers 4
    republic 99
Arabic x, 17, 82
Arabic-English Lexicon 82
Arabs 7, 46, 47, 108
    customary law of the 108
    minds of the 7
    unlettered 47
Arnold, Matthew 21, 56, 58
arts 8
Athenian(s) 3, 99
Athens 99, 100, 118
autocratic rulers 8
awliyā' 31

Balance, the 30, 36, 49, 54, 57,
    65
Baghdad 95
Barbarians 118
barzakh 85
believers 31
Bible 28
biological process 92
biologists 14
Bolshevism 120
bourgeoisie 119

Bridges, J.H. 27, 28
brotherhood 3, 17
   universal 15
bu'd (distance from God) 79
Bukhārī, al- viii, 3, 5, 15, 52, 65, 75, 83, 84

capitalism x
Carlyle 62, 67
catholicity 15, 17
Children of Adam 23
China 33
Chinese 28
Christ vii, 60, 120, 122
Christian 27, 28, 81, 120
   theologians 48
Christianity 12, 15, 35, 62
   European 120
civilization ix, xi 35, 112, 115-121
Civilizations 115, 116
Clarke 44
Cold war vi
Communism x
Comte 27
conduct, standard of 10, 95
Confucius 28
creation 11, 14, 20, 21, 23, 25, 30, 35, 36, 47, 50, 51, 62, 64, 67, 87, 91, 98, 112
   purpose of 23
cruelty 66
culture 35, 65, 112-117

Dark Ages 12
Day of Judgement 71, 76, 78, 83, 87, 103, 126
death 11, 44, 67, 72, 73, 78-80, 86, 88, 90, 91, 93, 127
   basic stage of preparation 91
   second period in the life of man 90
   not the end of life 11
   as a biological event 88
democracy viii, ix, 3, 4, 98, 99, 102, 105, 107, 118
democratic vii, 98, 99, 102, 107, 110, 118
dhimmī 103
dialectic 48
dictatorship 98, 107
dishonesty 66
divine, Activity 29
   Attribute 29, 32
   Countenance 96
   Decrees 45
   Mercy 86
   scheme of things 31
   Unity 12, 13, 17, 19, 20
   Veto 61
   Will 62
divinity 6
   essence of 29
Durr al-Manthūr, al- 85

Earth ix, 8, 20-25, 29, 30, 32-34, 36, 41, 49-51, 54, 61, 68, 74, 76, 78, 79, 82, 86, 87, 92, 94, 110, 113, 120-122

Index

East 12, 43, 94, 129
Egypt 1, 28
élite 8
Empedocles 56, 58, 59
English xii, 28, 37, 81, 82
esoteric meaning 7, 48
Europe 12, 119-121
European, civilization 35
   critics 43
   nations 122
   thinkers 119
evil x, 31, 38, 44, 52, 58-60, 66, 70-72, 79, 82, 83, 122, 125, 127, 130
evolutionary process 90

falsehood 66
Farewell Address 6
Fath al-Bārī 85
Fath al-Bayān 85
fatalism 45, 46
Fawz al-Akbar 90
fiqh 46, 106, 108, 109
fitrat Allāh 46, 47, 57
Fire 75, 77, 84, 88, 94, 105, 123
forgiveness 43, 52, 66, 71, 76, 80, 85, 86, 128, 129
fornication 66

geneticists 14
Gethsmane 60
ghāfilīn 31
Ghazālī 1, 38, 40
God, attributes of 29, 36
   a 'Pitiless tyrant' 43

Children of vii
Family of vii, 3, 13, 19, 25, 36, 66, 112
His knowledge of everything 57
journey to 39, 40
Kingdom of 120, 121
Republic of 100
return to 26
Rope of 6
Signs of 78
sovereignty belongs to 98
unity of x, 12, 16, 18-20, 26, 92
Will of 33, 42, 46, 51, 58, 67
Goethe 35, 62
Good viii, 18, 19, 25, 27, 32, 33, 44, 56-59, 61, 62, 66, 71, 72, 79, 82-84, 87, 95, 110, 113, 123, 125, 127-130
good intention 61
government viii, 107
   method of 98
Great Master 2
Greece 21, 48, 118, 119
Greek, civilization 118
   culture 35
Greeks 118

Hādī al-Arwāh 85
hadīth, genuine 5
   literature 5, 74, 109
   manufacturers of 5
   narrators of the 5

ḥadīth al-qudsī 75, 83
ḥalāl (lawful) 66
Hamlet 115
ḥarām (unlawful) 66
hate 66, 131
Heaven 21, 22, 32, 75-81, 84, 85, 103, 127, 128
  Gardens of 75
Heavens 20, 21, 23, 30, 34, 50, 61, 76, 82, 94
Hebrew 28
Hell 75-86
Hellenes 118, 119
Hellenic 120
Hellos 118
Hijrah 101, 106, 108
Hinduism 12
homo sapiens 14
ḥukm ilāhī 106, 107
human, action 43, 65
  dignity 13
  experience 37
  history 12, 105
  life x, 29, 54, 64, 85, 114, 120
  nature 3, 4, 13, 24, 115
humanity ix, 13, 19, 44, 105, 109, 110, 116-119, 121, 122
humility viii
ḥuqūb 82
ḥuqūq al-'ibād 64-68, 71, 100
ḥuqūq Allāh 64, 65, 67, 68, 71, 100, 101, 111
ḥuqūq an-nās 64, 68, 100, 101, 111

huzur al-qalb 94
hypocrisy 66

Ibn al-Qayyūm 85
Ibn Khallikan 5
Ibn Maskwaih 90
ijmā' 99
ijtihād 99, 106, 109
'ilm al-kalām 48
imperialists viii
indecency 66
India xii, 12
Industrial Revolution 119
injustice 49, 83, 128
intellectual 8, 12, 34, 50, 64, 66, 67, 119
Iqbāl, Sir Muḥammad 35, 36, 88, 89, 91
Isaac 17
Islam, Prophet of vii, 3, 32, 33, 122
  as an educational force 35
  cardinal belief in 26, 73
  early centuries of 43
  first state in 97
  foundations of the medieval 46
  God in 30
  history of 40, 108
  of the masses 7
  of the Middle Ages 7
  of the Qur'an 7
  positive sins in 66
  prayer(s) in 28, 124-131
  schismatic life for 4
  seventy-two sects of 4

Index

Islamic, history 41
   society 43
Ismāʿīl vii, 17
Israelite(s) 98, 107
Iḥyā' al-'Ulūm 1

jabriyyah 43
Jacob 17
Jerusalem 104
Jesus 16, 17
Jew 102, 103
jihād 59, 60, 104
jihād al-akbar, al- 59
Judaic 27, 81, 109
Judaism 15
justice, moral 61

kāfir 19
kāfirīn 31
Kanzul Ummal 84
khalq Allāh 46, 47, 57
khayr 66
Khilāfah 4, 43, 102
kindliness 66
King Lear ix
kitāb viii, 3, 15, 33, 48, 49, 52, 65, 74, 75, 79, 83-85, 104
kitāb wal hikmah 48-49
knowledge xi, xii, 18, 22, 28, 29, 32-34, 36, 37, 41, 42, 53, 57, 61, 72, 77, 107, 108, 118, 125, 128-130
   dynamic source of 41
   in the Qur'anic conception 34
   of 'Nature of things 37

   realm of 118
kufr 19, 59
   no compromise with 19

Lā ilāha illallāh 12, 20
Lane, E.W. 82
language, of God 17
   of the Qur'an 14, 36, 80, 90
Latin 27
law, of life 52, 56, 59, 67, 121, 122
   benevolent 50
   supremacy of 99
laws, of nature 50, 54, 57
League of Nations vii
life beautiful 81
life hereafter 25, 73, 74, 77, 92, 93
Lord of Compassion 57

madhāhib 106
Madīnah 1, 3, 102
Magian 109
majdhūb 40
Makkah 1, 6
malā'ikah 20, 21
man, disunity of 14
   emancipation of 13, 123
   made in the best of moulds 21
   nature of 52, 54, 57, 91
   origin of 90
   unity of x, 12, 13, 15, 18-20, 26, 92
mankind vii, ix, 3, 4, 8, 9,

13-15, 18, 25, 27, 41, 47, 49, 77, 95, 96, 110-114, 116, 117, 119, 121-123
Mathnawī 77
medieval, commentators of the Qur'an 19
mind 8, 74
Muslim History 8
Muslim theologian(s) 8, 45
metaphors 74
Middle Ages 7, 45, 119
mīzān 49
Mohammad (Prophet) 27, 85
Mohammed (Prophet) 44, 45
monarchy 4
moral purification 29
morality 29, 62
Moses 16, 17
Most Gracious 30, 71
Most Merciful 52, 71, 84, 86
mu'minīn 31
Muḥammad vii, viii, 12, 33, 35, 36, 65, 75, 88, 89, 91
muflihīn 31, 33, 97
mufsidīn 31
muhkamāt 6, 46, 49, 53
muhsinīn 31, 33
munāfiqīn 31
mundane 7, 69, 124
muqarribīn 31
muqsitīn 31, 33, 97
murder 14
mushrikīn 31
Muslihīn 31, 33
Muslim viii, xi, 1, 3, 7-9, 19, 33, 43-46, 48, 59, 67, 68, 70, 71, 74, 75, 79, 83, 84, 88, 99, 103, 104, 106, 107, 109, 110, 124-127
community 99
country 7
homes 7
religious thought 43
State 106
thinkers 88
thought and history 7
world 8
muslimīn 31, 33
Mussalman 27
mutashābihāt 6, 46, 48, 49, 74
muttaqīn 31, 36, 68, 97
mystic 7, 37-39, 41, 48, 77, 88, 95, 125
mystical 38
mysticism 29
function of 39

nafs 77
nationalism ix, x, 119, 123
nations vii-ix, 3, 15, 18, 32, 52, 97, 110, 113, 122
Nazism 120
Negro 2, 3, 8, 9, 95
neo-Platonic 109
neo-Platonism 7
Nestorian 109
new world order 41
Noah 16
non-Muslim 3, 19, 59
minorities 103

Index

Oft-forgiving 47, 52, 85, 86

Palgrave 43, 44
parables 74
Paradise 76, 82, 95
patience 60
philosophy 8, 44, 48, 113
Pir-e-Rumi 89
plants 35, 88, 89
Plato 118, 119
political, institutions 1
    interests 8
pre-determination 43
Preaching of Islam, The 104
proletariat 119
Prophet, Companions of the 85, 97
    life of the 7, 8, 45
    his vision of one world ix
    name of the 4
    prayer of the 34
    traditions of the 5
psychologists 14
Pythagoras 28

qadariyyah 43
qalb 38, 94
Qur'an, allegorical or figurative element in 6
    as a code of human conduct 10
    attitude towards other faith 19, 85
    commandments of 5, 101
    criticism of the 44
    does not use any technical terms 9
    economic system formulated by the 103
    faith of the x, 6
    is read parrot-like 7
    leading theme of the 15
    manner of presentation in the 6
    people of the 17
    phraseology of the 50
    promises salvation 17
    purpose of the 1, 10, 35, 45, 46, 89, 107
    teachings of the 2, 70
    the world purpose 1
    universality of the 1
    warning against sinful life 85
Qur'anic xi, 2, 4, 6-8, 17, 19, 28, 31, 34, 35, 40, 42, 45, 48, 50-53, 58, 59, 65, 74, 79, 81, 90, 99, 100, 103, 106, 107, 110
    concept of *Tawhīd* 81
    concept of the 'Will of God' 45
    ideals 4
    message 6
    notions of justice 100
    phraseology 7
    style 52
    un- 8, 107
qurb (nearness to God) 37, 79
qurb ilāhi 39

race ix, 13, 14, 27, 76, 121

Rāshidūn 98, 99, 101, 102, 105-107
Rāshidūnian 107, 108
Rāzī, Imām Fakhruddīn 76
reality 19, 28, 37-41, 57, 59, 60, 67, 74, 75, 93, 94, 113
religion x, xii, 7, 8, 10, 15, 16, 24, 27, 28, 35, 51, 100, 104, 106, 124
    standard 25, 46, 47
religiosity 1
religious life 8
Renaissance 119
repentance 52
Resurrection 11, 62, 86, 91
    Church of the 104
revelation 35, 49, 114
Right Religion 51
righteous work 11, 20, 24, 26, 65-67, 73, 92
rights, of God 64
    of the external world of creation 64
Roman 76, 99, 119, 120
    Empire 119
Rome 21, 118, 119
Rūmī, Jalāluddin 38, 77, 88-92

Sabians 18
ṣābirīn 31, 60, 68
ṣādiqīn 31, 97
ṣāliḥīn ix, x, 31, 33, 36, 68, 97, 100
Saul 98
sciences 8

scientific 5, 7, 89, 90, 108, 120
    doctrine 14
    fact 14
    method 45
scientists 14
Scripture 18, 48, 125
Scriptures 17
secularism x
Semetic 15
shākirīn 31
sharī'ah 106, 107
sharr 66
shuhadā' 31
shūrā 16, 20, 43, 56, 80, 93, 99, 100
ṣiddīqīn 31, 33, 36, 97
social, and political institutions 1
    and religious life 8
    relations 13, 115
society 3, 28, 33, 39, 40, 43, 54, 66, 68, 71, 75, 94, 96, 101, 109, 115-117, 124
    obligations to 65, 100, 101
sociologists 14
sovereignty (of a state) 98
Soviet Russia viii
sperm 87
spiritual, needs 4
    salvation 29
spirituality x
St John 22
'stage to stage' 11, 23, 54, 78, 81, 86, 88, 90
steadfastness 62, 72, 130

Index

Ṣūfī 38, 95
sunnah (of the Prophet) 106
sunnat al-'Arab 108
sunnat Allāh 27, 46, 47, 50, 57, 71, 108
Supreme Will 28, 70, 126
Syria 105

Tafsīr al-Kabīr, al- 76
taqdīr 56-60
tawhīd 52, 81, 83, 84
tawwābīn 33
teutonic 120
theocracy 28, 98, 100, 106, 107
theologians ix, 45, 46, 48, 83
Thomas Arnold, Sir 104-105
Tintern Abbey 39, 40
tolerance viii, 19, 58
treachery 66
truth ix, 12, 16, 21, 22, 24, 33, 44, 49, 54, 60, 62, 66, 69, 72, 92, 114, 120, 124, 130

'ulamā', reactionary 8
ūlu'l-'ilm 31, 32
ūlu'l-absār 68
ūlu'l-albāb 31, 68
'Umar, Caliph 1-3, 8, 85, 102-104
ummah 99, 101, 109
ummatun wasaṭ 97, 106, 107, 109, 111
Ummayyid(s) 4, 43
UNESCO 14
unfaithfulness 66
United Nations vii, viii, ix
Charter of the 3
Universal Declaration of Human Rights 3
universe ix, 34, 35, 47, 54
universities 3, 118
unseen 35, 61
USA viii
'Uthmān 102

vicegerency 23, 24, 29, 36, 92
vicegerent(s) of God ix, 24, 25, 30, 32, 40, 41

Wadia, Ardaser Sorabjee N. 45
West 12, 94, 129
Western 27, 119
William Muir, Sir 44, 45

ẓalimīn 31
Zoroastrian 45
Zoroastrianism 76